THE GOSPEL WRECKING CREW

WRECK RELIGION. REDISCOVER THE REAL JESUS.
A GUIDE FOR THOSE WHO LEFT THE CHURCH.

JOE DEGIDIO

TABLE OF CONTENTS

WHY READ THIS BOOK?

This book is not for everyone. In fact, if you are a lifelong churchgoer who has never once questioned what you've been told, who nods along every Sunday and feels completely at peace with the version of Jesus handed to you by your pastor, your priest, or your denomination — put this down. It will only frustrate you.

But if you're still reading, there's a good chance this book was written for you.

If you walked away from church — or were quietly pushed out — and never looked back, read this book. If you tried religion and found it hollow, performative, or worse, hypocritical, read this book. If you sat through one too many sermons that answered nothing, if you watched the fog machine roll across the stage and thought, *there has to be more than this*, read this book.

If you're not sure you believe in God at all — if you're an atheist, an agnostic, or someone who lands somewhere in the uncomfortable middle — I am not here to ambush you. I only ask that you read the first three chapters with an open mind. That's all. What you do after that is entirely up to you.

If you are carrying something heavy right now — a diagnosis, a loss, a marriage falling apart, a child you can't reach, a life that isn't turning out the way you planned — and you need to know whether there is a God who actually gives a damn about any of it, read this book.

If you've been told that God is punishing you, that your suffering is your fault, that the cancer or the tragedy or the heartbreak is somehow divine retribution for your failures, read this book. That is not the God I found in the first century, and it is not the God I am going to introduce you to here.

If you think Jesus is a political figure, a mascot for a particular party, a weapon wielded by people who seem angrier than they are loving — read this book. What they've done to his name and his message should offend all of us.

If you're a new Christian who was handed a pamphlet and told, *"You're saved — see you Sunday,"* and have been quietly confused ever since, read this book.

And if you've spent years — maybe decades — trying to be good enough, holy enough, obedient enough to earn something from God, and you're exhausted from the effort, *please* read this book. Because the first-century gospel has a word for you, and that word is: *stop.* You never had to earn it. You never could. That's the whole point.

This book won't ask you to join anything, tithe anything, or perform anything. It will ask you to think — and to consider the possibility that the Jesus you were sold is not the Jesus who actually showed up two thousand years ago and turned the world upside down.

That Jesus is still out there. This book is about finding him.

WHY DID I WRITE
THIS BOOK?

Because I am not a pastor. I am not a theologian. I am a guy who was sitting in a bible study the day a pastor died on a mission trip, and the best answer our mega church could offer his grieving wife and kids was: *"God took him."*

That answer nearly cost me my faith. It also made me angry enough to start asking better questions.

Think about what that phrase does to a person. If God took him — if God looked down at a faithful man serving others and decided to snatch him away, leaving his wife and children behind — then what kind of God are we dealing with? A capricious one. A cruel one. One that honest people should want nothing to do with. I almost walked away that day. And I would not have been wrong to.

But something didn't sit right. Not with that answer, and not with the casual confidence with which it was delivered. So I started digging — not into theology, but into history. Into what ordinary people in the first century actually understood about God before the institutions got involved. What I found stunned me.

The instructional material available to people genuinely searching for answers is, to put it plainly, abysmal. I know this firsthand. I was once sent to participate in an Alpha program at our mega church — one of the most widely used introductory Christianity courses in the world. A man showed up who had just been diagnosed with MS. He asked, and desperately, *"How do I get more faith?"* He asked it three times. Not one of the program leaders answered him. I finally told him that faith is something you build, not something you go out and get — and pointed him to the parable of the man who built his house on a rock. That was enough to get me asked to leave.

That moment stayed with me. If the best-resourced churches in the country can't answer a sick man's most basic question, something is broken. Not in him. In the material.

So I wrote this book to fix that — at least in part. To compress thirty years of accumulated understanding into something a regular person can actually use. To answer the questions that churches dodge on Sundays: Why do bad things happen to good people? Why doesn't God stop the suffering? What does faith actually mean, and how do you get more of it? When I die, is this the end of me?

I am not trying to convert you. A book can't do that, and I wouldn't try. What I am trying to do is hand you the first-century message — stripped of 2,000 years of institutional baggage — and let you decide what to do with it.

I hope it's enough to make at least you curious.

PROLOGUE

It is 34 AD. There are no churches.

There are no pastors, no priests, no cardinals, no popes. There are no stained glass windows, no collection plates, no fog machines, no Sunday bulletins. There is no New Testament. There is no Christian radio, no televangelists, no mega-church welcome centers sizing up your net worth before you've found your seat.

There is only a message.

And that message is spreading like a brushfire.

It started in Jerusalem, in the chaotic aftermath of a public execution that didn't end the way anyone expected. A small group of people — fishermen, tax collectors, outcasts, women whose testimony wasn't even considered valid in a court of law — began telling anyone who would listen that something had happened. Something that changed everything. Not a new religion. Not a new set of rules. A new reality. God, they said, was no longer distant. No longer barricaded behind temple walls and priestly gatekeepers and elaborate systems of sacrifice and debt. He had torn all of that down. He was reachable. Personal. And he was pursuing *you* — not because of what you had done, but despite it.

That was the message. That was all of it.

No membership required. No rituals to perform. No social or political agenda to sign onto. Just an outstretched hand from a God who, against all expectation and all religious logic, turned out to be on your side.

Within a generation, that message had traveled from Jerusalem to

Antioch, from Antioch to Greece, from Greece to Rome — the very capital of the empire that had tried to silence it. It crossed borders without passports and went viral without the internet. It reached slaves and senators, merchants and soldiers, the powerful and the utterly forgotten. It spread because the people who heard it could not keep it to themselves. Many of them paid for that with their lives. And they considered it a fair trade.

Now ask yourself: what happened to *that* Christianity?

Somewhere in the 2,000 years between then and now, something went badly wrong. The come-as-you-are message became a dress code. The guilt-free invitation became a ledger of sins. The God who pursued you became the God who punished you. The joyous, unstoppable movement of the first century got swallowed up — by empire, by institutions, by politics, by money — until what remained looked almost nothing like what it had started.

This book is an attempt to go back. Not to a building or a denomination, but to the message itself. The one that changed the world once.

It can change yours.

CHAPTER 1
THE LIKENESS OF BEING

Consider that there is a part of you that will not disappear when your body does. It is about the soul — what it is, why it matters, and why the restlessness you feel in quiet moments is not a malfunction but a signal. Before the book can go anywhere useful, it has to start here: with the question of what you actually are, and what you were made for. If you have ever sensed that there is more to you than biology, maybe there is an explanation.

Body, Soul & Spirit

Start with what you already know. You have a body. It is made of carbon, nitrogen, calcium, and water — the same basic materials that make up dust. The Bible says we came from dust and will return to it. Secular science agrees. Whatever you believe about God, on this point, everyone is aligned: the body is temporary.

But is that all you are?

Most people, if they're honest, don't think so. The concept of the soul runs so deep in human language and experience that we can't seem to get rid of it — soulmates, soul music, a troubled soul, an old soul. We speak of it constantly without stopping to ask what we mean. The soul is your conscience, your inner voice, the part of you that feels the weight of a moral decision even when no one is watching. You can't touch it. You can't weigh it. But you know it's there.

Theologians have long held that humans are three-part beings: body, soul, and spirit — and that each part is sustained by something different. The body is fed by food and responds to the physical world. An arrow will wound the body but leave the soul untouched. The soul, on the other hand, is fed by words, relationships, and meaning. The childhood saying that "words will never hurt me" is simply false. Words wound the soul deeply — and kind words heal it just as powerfully. The epistle of James put it plainly: "The tongue is a fire."

The spirit is something else again. It is the animating force behind your will — the thing that keeps a person alive against all medical odds, that drives someone across a marathon finish line when the body has nothing left, that gives life its sense of direction and purpose. The spirit is less about feeling and more about drive. When we say a team "has spirit," we mean something real, even if we can't fully define it.

Now here is where it gets interesting.

Physicist and philosopher Young-Hoon Kim has argued, drawing on quantum theory, that information is never created or destroyed — it simply exists, waiting to be discovered. Kim proposes that the soul is essentially information: like data stored in a cloud, it may leave the body at death, but it doesn't simply vanish. Consciousness, in his framework, exists independently of the brain. If he's right, then your existence has three phases — before the body, inside the body, and after the body — and the middle part, the one you're living right now, is the briefest of the three.

Plato intuited something similar, centuries before quantum

physics existed. In the *Phaedo*, he compared the soul to a musical piece. The music doesn't cease to exist because no one is playing it — it exists independently, waiting for an instrument. The body is the instrument. The spirit is the force that draws the bow across the strings and brings the music to life. When the instrument decays, the music doesn't die with it. It simply waits.

What makes Jesus unique among the figures of history is that he is the only one who directly and specifically addresses what happens to that music after the instrument is gone, not in vague terms, not as poetry or metaphor, but as a concrete promise. That's a conversation we'll return to. For now, it's enough to sit with this: you are more than your body, and your body already knows it.

The Problem of Physics

There are laws you cannot break.

Drop a stone, and it falls—every time, without exception, without negotiation. The law of gravity does not care who you are, what you believe, or how badly you need the stone to stay in the air. It simply acts. The same is true for every physical law governing the universe — thermodynamics, electromagnetism, and the speed of light. Scientists have spent centuries probing these laws, testing their limits, searching for exceptions. They haven't found any. The laws hold. They always hold.

Now here is the question worth sitting with: who made them?

If you believe the universe simply *happened* — that the laws of physics emerged from nothing, by accident, with no author — that is a coherent position, and this book isn't going to argue you out of it in a single chapter. But if you're even open to the possibility that someone designed the physical laws, then a second question follows almost immediately: did that same someone design laws governing something other than physics?

Consider what you already know about human beings. We are not purely physical creatures — we established that in the last section. We have a soul, a conscience, an inner moral sense that operates independently of gravity and thermodynamics. And that moral sense appears to be governed by something. There are patterns to it. Betrayal damages trust — every time. Dishonesty, left unchecked, compounds — always. Cruelty corrodes the person practicing it as surely as it wounds the person receiving it. These are not random outcomes. They are consistent, predictable, and universal. They behave, in other words, like laws.

The Bible calls these the fruits of the Spirit — the visible outcomes of living in alignment or misalignment with the way human beings were designed to function. But you don't have to be a Christian to recognize them. You don't need a church, a creed, or even a belief in God to notice that certain behaviors produce certain consequences with something close to mathematical regularity. Cultures that have never encountered the Bible have still independently arrived at prohibitions against murder, theft, and betrayal. Something in the human conscience already knew.

Here is where the physics analogy becomes useful — and where it also breaks down in an important way.

Physical laws are involuntary. You cannot choose to ignore gravity. But spiritual laws are different. They don't compel; they *invite*. You can choose to be unfaithful. You can choose to lie, to steal, to cultivate bitterness. The law won't stop you. But the consequences will arrive just the same — not as divine punishment delivered from above, but as the natural, inevitable outcome of how the universe is structured. Unfaithfulness doesn't just damage a marriage; it rewires the person who practices it, making the next act of betrayal easier and pulling them further and further from the person they were meant to be. The drift is slow at first. Then it isn't.

This is what makes spiritual laws more demanding than physical ones, not less. Gravity requires nothing of you. Spiritual laws require everything — your attention, your choices, your daily decisions about which direction you're going to move. And unlike a stone, you can move either way.

The first-century Christians understood this intuitively. The message of grace they carried wasn't a license to ignore the spiritual laws — it was the announcement that when you inevitably failed to keep them, as every human being does, there was a way back. The drift could be reversed. The distance could be closed, not by trying harder, but by something far more radical than effort.

That's what the rest of this book is about.

Seat of Justice

Here is something most of us would rather not admit: we want justice for everyone except ourselves.

When someone cuts me off in traffic, I want consequences. When a coworker takes credit for work they didn't do, I want accountability. When I read about fraud, corruption, or cruelty in the news, something in me demands that the scales get balanced. We are, all of us, deeply and instinctively committed to justice — right up until the moment it turns in our direction.

Because here is my morning, most mornings.

I'm on my way to work, and someone cuts me off. The finger goes up before I've even thought about it. I get to the office, and it's expense report day — I'm short a few receipts, so my creative instincts take over, and the numbers get quietly massaged. My son calls and says something I don't like, and I bite his head off. It's 9 AM. I've broken three or four spiritual laws before my first cup of coffee is cold, and I haven't given them a second thought.

Now I want God to be just. Just with the corrupt politician. Just with the person who wronged my friend. Just with the genuinely wicked people of the world. But just with *me*? I couldn't help it. My emotions got the better of me. You know how it is.

A God who plays favorites with his justice, however, is not a just God. He is a corrupt one. Real justice doesn't make exceptions for good intentions or extenuating circumstances. It levels the playing field — for Mother Teresa and for Stalin, for the person who wronged you and for you. If God is genuinely just, then my 9 AM offenses are on the ledger too, right alongside everything I've been shaking my fist at.

Our ancestors recognized this problem and sought to solve it through sacrifice—goats, first fruits, burnt offerings — some transaction that might tip the scales back toward balance. But think about how strange that logic is. You've violated a spiritual law. The breach is between you and a perfect God. And your proposed remedy is to hand back something God created and gave you in the first place. It's like cheating on someone and then offering them their own Christmas gift as an apology. The gesture doesn't reach the wound.

So we moved on from animal sacrifice to something more modern: the apology. The mea culpa. *I'm so sorry —it will never happen again*—which, if we're being honest, lasts until the next time someone cuts us off in traffic. We confess. We drift. We confess again. Rinse and repeat. The problem isn't the sincerity of the confession. The problem is that sincere confession, repeated daily and followed by the same behavior, doesn't actually settle anything. It just kicks the debt down the road.

And God, meanwhile, doesn't seem to be doing anything about it. No lightning bolt. No immediate consequence. You sped through the school zone and got home fine. You massaged the expense report, and nobody noticed. The silence can feel like permission — or worse, like indifference. It makes it very easy to keep drifting, a little further each day, away from the God you claim to believe in. The distance accumulates quietly, the way debt does when you stop opening the statements.

This is the problem of justice — not the dramatic, headline-grabbing kind, but the mundane, daily, 9 AM kind. The gap between the person we intend to be and the person we actually are by the time we reach the office. Between the standard we demand of others and the grace we demand for ourselves.

Here is what makes Christianity different from every other answer to this problem: it doesn't ask you to close the gap through effort. It doesn't offer a better sacrifice, a more sincere confession, or a stricter moral regimen. It offers something far more unexpected — and far more unsettling.

But we're not quite there yet.

An Easy Walk

Walking away from God is not a dramatic event. There is no declaration, no door slamming, no moment you can point to and say: *that's when it happened.* It happens quietly, incrementally, one small substitution at a time — and the reason it's so easy is that the replacements feel perfectly adequate, at least at first.

Your soul was built to be connected to something. That is not a religious statement — it is simply an observation about how human beings function. We need input, truth, a sense of meaning, and a source of hope that doesn't depend on how the week is going. When that connection to God goes dark, the soul doesn't sit empty. It can't. It reaches for whatever is available, and the world is more than happy to offer candidates.

So your truth becomes whatever narrative you've been consuming

— the news cycle, the algorithm, the voices that confirm what you already suspect and stoke what you already fear. Your freedom becomes a long weekend that still somehow leaves you exhausted. Your satisfaction becomes the quiet scorecard you keep against your neighbors, your colleagues, your old classmates — a game with no finish line and no winner. Your peace becomes the performance of being fine, of holding it together in public, of saying *I'm good* when someone asks, even when you're not.

And for a while, it works. Or it seems to.

But the soul is not easily fooled for long. The substitutes start to show their limits. The news makes you angrier, not calmer. The accomplishments feel hollow the morning after. The performance of contentment requires more energy every year to maintain. And underneath all of it, something accumulates — a low-grade dissatisfaction that you can't quite name, a restlessness that doesn't respond to the usual remedies. You start stuffing it down. You get better at stuffing it down. Until one day the bucket is full, and the overflow lands on the people closest to you — the ones who were never the problem — because they're the only ones you trust enough to stop pretending around.

This is not a crisis. It doesn't look like one from the outside. It looks like a normal life. And that is precisely what makes it so dangerous.

Because here is what's actually happening beneath the surface: your soul is drifting. Not falling — drifting. Slowly, without drama, further and further from the source it was designed to connect to. And the longer the drift continues, the more normal the distance feels, until one day the idea of closing it seems not just difficult but faintly absurd. *I'm fine. I don't need that.*

Now the question of eternity enters the room.

If your soul is real — and we've already established that most people, even those who claim not to believe in one, act as though it is — then the question of where it ends up matters enormously. Not abstractly. Personally. You are going somewhere. The drift has a direction. And if eternal life means anything, it means connection — to God, to the people you love, to something larger and more permanent than anything this world has offered you so far. A soul floating untethered through eternity, disconnected from all of that, is not paradise. It's not a bowling alley in Gary, Indiana, either — but it's not where you want to be.

If you believe your life simply *ends* — that the last breath is the period at the end of the sentence and there is nothing after — then, in the most important sense, you are already treating yourself as a dead man walking and going through the motions and managing the days. I'm not saying that to be harsh. I'm saying it because the stakes are real, and the drift is quiet, and most people don't realize how far they've gone until something forces them to look up and take their bearings.

Suppose it's not a circle. Suppose it's a straight, infinite line — and you are already on it, moving in one direction or the other, right now, today.

That changes things.

How Much for Your Soul?

Here is a simple experiment. Someone offers you two dollars to sign a piece of paper. The paper says you are selling your soul. There's a disclaimer at the bottom — *this is not a legally binding contract* — and you can tear it up the moment you sign it and keep the money. Two dollars. No strings. No consequences.

Would you sign it?

Social psychologists at the University of Virginia put this exact question to a group of college students. The students were largely self-identified atheists and agnostics — people who, by their own account, didn't believe they had a soul to sell. And yet when the paper was placed in front of them, only 23% signed. Three out of four people who claimed not to believe in a soul refused to sell the one they didn't have, for two dollars, with a disclaimer, knowing they could immediately destroy the evidence.

Stephen Dubner, the host of the Freakonomics podcast, spent nearly a decade running his own informal version of the same experiment. He raised his offer to fifty dollars. He debated committed atheists. He made the case, repeatedly, that if the soul doesn't exist, the transaction is meaningless — essentially free money. Nobody signed. He managed to purchase one man's Dignity and several people's sense of Humor. Not a single soul changed hands.

What do we do with that?

At a minimum, it tells us something that pure reason cannot quite account for. There is something in the human being — even the skeptical, secular, thoroughly modern human being — that treats the soul as real, as precious, as not for sale at any price, even when the conscious mind has officially concluded it doesn't exist. You can argue yourself out of the belief intellectually. But something deeper isn't listening.

Solomon noticed this three thousand years ago. In Ecclesiastes, he wrote that God has set eternity in the human heart — that there is something woven into us that reaches toward the permanent, the infinite, the things that do not end. Not as a religious instinct, but as a fundamental feature of what we are. We are the only creatures that build monuments to our dead. The only ones that ask *what happens after*. The only ones for whom the idea of simply ceasing to exist feels, at some deep level, like a violation of something.

Here is why this matters practically, not just philosophically.

You are getting older. The people you love are getting older. The window of time in which these questions feel abstract and deferrable is shorter than it appears. And if your soul is real — if the 77% of students who wouldn't sign that paper were responding to something genuine — then the question of where it is going, and what it is connected to, and whether there is a God who actually knows your name, is not a question you can afford to keep kicking down the road indefinitely.

The road has an end. And as Solomon also put it: no one can fathom what God has done from beginning to end. But knowing who holds the beginning and the end is, as it turns out, enough.

On Our Own

There is a growing segment of the American population that researchers call the "nones" — not nuns, but n-o-n-e-s. They are people who, when asked about their religious affiliation, check the box that says *none*. No church, no creed, no denomination. The Pew Research Center estimates they make up roughly 23% of Americans, and the number is climbing, particularly among younger adults. They are not, for the most part, hardened atheists. Most of them believe in something — some God, some force, some organizing principle behind the universe. They just haven't signed up with anyone.

And most of them have a plan.

The plan goes something like this: *I'm a good person. I treat people fairly. I don't steal, I don't cheat, I'm kind to my neighbors, and I show up for the people I love. Whatever God is out there, surely he can see that. Surely that counts for something.* It's a reasonable-sounding position. It's also, if you think it through carefully, built on a foundation that collapses the moment you apply any pressure to it.

Here's the pressure.

Picture a line of people arranged from left to right — most virtuous on the left, most monstrous on the right. Start with Mother Teresa on the far left. Then Oprah. Then the Pope. Then Michael Jordan. Then Donald Trump. Then Paul McCartney. Then Nancy Pelosi. Then Aaron Rodgers. Then Stalin. Then Hitler on the far right.

Now take a pen and draw a vertical line somewhere in that lineup — everyone to your left is going to heaven, everyone to your right is going to hell. Where do you draw it?

Go ahead. Take a moment.

The first problem is obvious: you want to argue with the order right away. Maybe Trump belongs closer to Hitler in your view, or maybe Pelosi does, depending on your politics. Maybe you don't think overpaid quarterbacks deserve to be anywhere near Mother Teresa. The moment you start rearranging the lineup, you've demonstrated the first flaw in the "good enough" plan — the standard is entirely subjective. Everyone draws the line in a different place, and everyone draws it in a place that puts themselves safely on the heaven side. Conveniently.

The second problem is deeper. Who gave you the pen?

This is the question the "good enough" approach never answers. It assumes that the standard for entry is relative — that what matters is being better than a meaningful number of others. But a God who is truly just doesn't grade on a curve. He can't. A God who looks at the lineup and says *well, you're no Stalin, so you're fine* is not a just God — he is an arbitrary one, which is arguably worse. Real justice, as we established earlier, is absolute. It doesn't adjust based on who else is in the room.

From God's perspective, according to every tradition that takes him seriously, the lineup doesn't sort into the good side and the bad side. The whole lineup misses the mark. Mother Teresa said so herself — she wrote extensively about her own sense of falling short, of the gap between who she was and who she was called to be. If she felt the gap, what does that say about the rest of us?

We never apply this logic to our earthly relationships and expect it to work. You don't show up to a job interview and say, "Well, I'm more qualified than most people who aren't applying for this job." You don't tell a judge, *your honor, relative to some people I could name, I'm practically a saint.* The comparison game only feels persuasive when we're the ones holding the pen and drawing the line.

Here is the uncomfortable conclusion: if getting right with God depends on being good enough, then none of us are making it. Not the nones. Not the churchgoers. Not the people who tithe every week, volunteer every Saturday, and haven't missed a Sunday service in twenty years. The standard, properly understood, is perfection — and perfection is not on offer from any human being who has ever lived.

Which means the "good enough" plan isn't a plan at all. It's a hope dressed up as a strategy.

And this is precisely where the first-century gospel becomes not just interesting, but urgent. Because the message those early Christians were willing to die for wasn't *"try harder," "be better,"* or *"do enough good things to tip the scales."* It was something far more radical than that. It was the announcement that the scales had already been balanced — not by anything you did, but by something done on your behalf, whether you deserved it or not.

You didn't. That's the whole point.

Gunning For Pursuit

There are a handful of things in life that feel genuinely satisfying — not just pleasant, but *validating* in a way that goes deeper than the moment—getting something right after working hard at it. A meal that actually delivers on its promise. And being pursued.

Being pursued is interesting because of what it does to you internally. It tells you that someone saw you — really saw you — and decided you were worth the effort of crossing the distance. It doesn't matter who you are or how put-together you appear on the outside. Most of us carry a private suspicion that if people really knew us — the 9 AM version of us, the 2 AM version of us — they would quietly reconsider. Being pursued by someone who knows all of that and comes anyway is a different thing entirely. It is, if you let it be, one of the most disorienting and transformative experiences available to a human being.

Which is why what comes next is so extraordinary.

After everything we've covered in this chapter — the soul drifting, the spiritual laws broken before breakfast, the "good enough" plan that isn't good enough, the scales of justice that nobody can balance on their own — the response from God is not what most people expect. It is not a list of requirements. It is not a warning. It is not a cold shoulder earned by all the distance we've put between ourselves and him.

It is a pursuit.

Not a polite invitation extended to the people who have it mostly together. A pursuit — active, personal, reaching across whatever distance exists — aimed specifically at the ones who are weary. The ones who are burdened. The ones who have been trying to carry something they were never designed to carry alone, and who are running out of road.

Into that moment, a Jewish carpenter from Nazareth said this:

"Come to me, all you who are weary and burdened, and I will give you rest. Take my yoke upon you and learn from me, for I am gentle and humble in heart, and you will find rest for your souls. For my yoke is easy, and my burden is light." — Matthew 11:28-30

Three phrases. Each one is worth sitting with.

"Come to me — all of you."

The invitation is the first thing to notice, and the word *all* is the most important in it. Not some. Not the ones who qualify. Not the people who have cleaned themselves up enough to be presentable. All. That means the person who hasn't set foot in a church in twenty years. The one who is furious at God. The one who isn't sure God exists. The one who has done things they are certain put them beyond the reach of any reasonable forgiveness. The one who has been told, explicitly, by someone claiming to speak for Jesus, that people like them are not welcome.

He is not excluding anyone. If that is you — if you have been told that the door is closed to you — take your wrecking ball to that message because it did not come from him.

"Take my yoke upon you and learn from me."

In the ancient world, a yoke was a training tool — a frame that connected a young, untrained ox to an experienced one so the younger animal could learn the pace and direction from the older one. It was not a punishment. It was guidance. Jesus is not saying *carry my burden on top of your own.* He is saying, "Let me show you how to walk." Let me set the pace. Learn from me — not from the institution, not from the denomination, not from the celebrity pastor with the book deal — from me.

There is something beyond the fog machine and the Sunday performance that he is pointing toward. Something that requires no building, no membership, no correct political opinion. Just proximity to him, and the willingness to learn.

"You will find rest for your souls."

This is the part that either sounds like everything or like nothing, depending on where you are right now.

If your soul is at rest — if you have no unresolved conflicts eating at you, no bills keeping you up at night, no marriage straining under its own weight, no quiet sense that you are going through motions that stopped meaning anything years ago — then this promise may not land with much force. Come back to it later.

But if you know what soul-tiredness feels like. If you have been practicing contentment for so long that you've forgotten what the real thing feels like. If you are held together on the outside and quietly falling apart on the inside, then *rest for your soul* is not a small offer. It is, if he can actually deliver it, the most important thing anyone has ever said to you.

Notice what he does not say. He does not say, "fix yourself first, then come." He does not say: *light a candle, say a prayer, complete a program, attend a class, confess to a priest*. He says come. He says the yoke is easy. He says the burden is light. And then he puts himself on the line with a promise so specific and so audacious that if he cannot keep it, he is a fraud — and if he can, everything changes.

The rest of this book is about whether he can.

CHAPTER 2
WHAT A WORLD, WHAT A WORLD

"You cursed brat, look what you have done! I am melting, melting! Oh, what a world, what a world! Who would have thought a good little girl like you could destroy my beautiful wickedness?" The wicked Witch of the West.

As a tepid bucket of water wreaks acid-like havoc on the wicked witch of the west, she laments that a good little girl destroys her beautiful wickedness. There is a phrase buried in that famous death scene that is worth pulling out: *beautiful wickedness*. Not ugly wickedness. Not crude or accidental wickedness. Beautiful. Engineered. Precision-crafted to feel inevitable, to look like life, to pass as normal. If you were designing a trap, that is exactly how you would design it — not as something obviously terrible, but as something that feels almost right, almost satisfying, almost enough right up until it isn't.

Solomon, writing three thousand years ago in the book of Ecclesiastes, described the world with a word that stops you cold: meaningless. Not difficult. Not unfair. *Meaningless.* Everything comes and goes. Generations rise and fall and are forgotten. The sun makes its circuit. The rivers run to the sea, and the sea is never full. And then it happens again. And again. Nothing new under the sun.

That is either the most depressing thing you have ever read, or the most clarifying. Because if Solomon is right — and he was one of the wealthiest, wisest, most accomplished men who ever lived, a man who had tried everything the world offers and reported back honestly — then the feeling you have had, that low-grade suspicion that something is fundamentally off, is not a personal failure. It is an accurate diagnosis.

This chapter is about that diagnosis. And about what, if anything, can be done about it.

A Meaningless Prison

Ecclesiastes opens like a gut punch:

> *"Meaningless! Meaningless!" says the Teacher. "Utterly meaningless! Everything is meaningless. What do people gain from all their labors at which they toil under the sun? Generations come, and generations go, but the earth remains forever... All things are wearisome, more than one can say. The eye never has enough of seeing, nor the ear its fill of hearing. What has been will be again, what has been done will be done again; there is nothing new under the sun."*

Read that slowly. This is not a man who gave up too early. Solomon had wealth, power, wisdom, accomplishment, pleasure — everything the world tells you will be enough. He tried all of it. And his conclusion, after a lifetime of experience, was that it runs in circles.

Think about how the world is designed, if you were to design it from scratch as a kind of beautiful, wicked trap. You would want people to feel like they are making progress, so you give them upgrades — a better phone, a bigger house, a newer car — each one promising to be the thing that finally delivers. You would build in just enough genuine good — medicine, connection, moments of real beauty — to keep people from giving up entirely. You would make sure that as one disease is eradicated, another emerges. That as one injustice is addressed, another takes its place. The news cycle never runs out of material.

You would make sure people are remembered just long enough that legacy feels worth pursuing — then forgotten completely within two generations. You would design it so that death arrives unpredictably, keeps its timing secret, and often comes in the cruelest possible form.

Does that sound familiar? Does it sound designed?

Solomon thought so. And he was not wrong that it *feels* like a prison — a place where you work and strive and accumulate and lose, where the cycles repeat, and the meaning you were sure was just around the corner keeps receding. A place where, if you are honest, the escape fantasies are never far from the surface.

The question is: escape to what?

Wants Beget Regrets

Nobody plans to wreck their life. They just want things.

A bigger house. A newer car. A vacation that finally feels like enough. Sometimes a different spouse. The wanting feels productive — like motion, like progress. It isn't. It's an escape. And escape, by definition, means you're running from something.

The cycle is almost mechanical. You want something badly enough to go into debt for it. For a while, the having feels as good as the wanting promised to be. Then it doesn't. The novelty fades, the payments don't, and somewhere in the background, a low-grade disappointment sets in that you can't quite name. So you find the next thing to want. And the wheel keeps turning.

James — not an apostle, not a theologian, but Jesus' actual flesh-and-blood brother — watched this destroy people up close and wrote about it with zero sentimentality:

"What causes fights and quarrels among you? Don't they come from your desires that battle within you? You want something but don't get it. You kill and covet, but you cannot have what you want."

Read that again. He's not describing addicts or criminals. He's describing ordinary people — people who want reasonable things and can't understand why the wanting keeps making them miserable. The desire itself becomes the war. Not just against other people, but inside you. A battle between what you have, what you want, and the growing suspicion that getting it still won't be enough.

C.S. Lewis saw where that road ends. In *The Great Divorce*, he imagined hell not as fire and torment but as a city where everyone gets exactly what they want — instantly, effortlessly, just by thinking about it. No waiting. No negotiating. No need for anyone else.

At first, it sounds like paradise. It isn't.

Because when you never need anything from another person, you stop having anything to do with other people. The city keeps expanding — everyone moving further and further apart, building their dream house in some new empty quarter, alone with everything they ever wanted. Lewis's hell isn't punishment. It's the logical conclusion of a life organized entirely around your own desires. You get everything. You end up with nothing—nobody to share it with. Nobody needs you—just you, your stuff, and all the silence you could ever want.

That image should stop you cold. Because it's not just a picture of hell — it's a picture of a direction. A direction many people are already moving in, one reasonable want at a time.

So ask yourself the question underneath all the wanting: escape from what, exactly? Because if your life is something you need to escape from, the problem isn't that you don't have enough yet. The problem is what you're connected to — and what you're not.

Born of Frustration

Let's try a small experiment. Tomorrow morning, wake up and decide to be completely good. Not saintly — just good. No impatience. No cutting remarks. No quiet judgments about the driver in front of you, the colleague who talks too much, the family member who knows exactly which nerve to find—just one day of genuine, uninterrupted goodness.

See how long it lasts.

C.S. Lewis wasn't being cynical when he wrote, "No man knows how bad he is till he tries to be very good." He was being precise. The attempt itself exposes something. You don't discover your capacity for frustration, selfishness, or pettiness by reading about it. You discover it the moment you seriously try to stop.

This isn't a personality flaw. It isn't a willpower problem. It's structural. You were born into a world already tilted away from God, and that tilt is inside you whether you asked for it or not. The connection between humanity and God was severed long before you arrived — not because God abandoned us, but because we didn't trust him. We suspected the connection was more for his benefit than ours. That suspicion opened a door, and through it came everything this chapter has been describing: the grinding, the decay, the injustice, the death. Not as punishment. As a consequence.

And you inherited it. All of it.

Paul — brilliant, disciplined, deeply committed — sat down and wrote the most honest thing any religious person has ever written:

"I do not understand what I do. For what I want to do, I do not

do, but what I hate, I do. For I do not do the good I want to do, but the evil I do not want to do — this I keep on doing."

Sit with that for a second. This isn't a struggling newcomer finding his footing. This is the man who wrote half the New Testament, who planted churches across the ancient world, who stared down imprisonment and beatings and shipwrecks without flinching — and he couldn't stop doing the thing he hated. He wanted to be good. He tried to be good. And something in him kept pulling in the other direction anyway.

If it happened to Paul, it's happening to you. The apology you keep meaning to make. The habit you've quit a dozen times— the version of yourself you've been planning to become since the beginning of last year. The gap between who you intend to be and who you actually are on a Wednesday afternoon — that gap is not a personal failing. It is the human condition, and it has a name. This world handed it to you at birth, and it will be with you until something stronger than willpower intervenes.

The Hanoi Hilton

In 1965, U.S. Navy pilot James Stockdale was shot down over North Vietnam and taken prisoner. He would spend the next seven and a half years in the Hoa Lo Prison — known to American POWs as the Hanoi Hilton — enduring torture, isolation, and conditions designed to break men completely. He was the senior military officer among the prisoners. The weight of leadership fell to him.

He survived. Not just physically, but psychologically intact. And when author Jim Collins later asked him how, Stockdale's answer was not what most people expected. He did not credit optimism. In fact, he said the optimists were the ones who didn't make it.

The men who broke, Stockdale explained, were the ones who kept setting mental deadlines for their release. They convinced themselves they'd be home by Christmas. Then Easter. Then Thanksgiving. Then Christmas again. Each deadline came and went. Each one that passed without rescue took something out of them — until eventually, there was nothing left. They died, he said, of a broken heart.

What kept Stockdale himself intact was something harder and rarer: the ability to hold two things at once that most people cannot hold simultaneously. On one side, an absolute, unshakeable conviction that he would get out — that the story would not end in that prison. On the other, an equally unflinching willingness to look at his situation exactly as it was, without softening it, without pretending it was better than it was, without the false comfort of a deadline.

This has come to be called the Stockdale Paradox — the insight that genuine resilience is not optimism, and it is not realism. It is both at the same time, held in tension, neither one allowed to collapse into the other.

What is remarkable is that this is also, precisely, the posture Christianity asks of its followers. Not blind optimism — the world will get better, things will work out, good people are rewarded. The New Testament is brutally honest about the world: it is broken, it will remain broken, suffering is real and guaranteed, and not always explainable. But underneath that brutal honesty runs an unshakable conviction: this is not how the story ends.

The American Psychological Association defines hope not as wishful thinking but as the expectation that positive outcomes are possible — a forward-leaning orientation toward the future even in the face of current suffering. Stockdale had that. The first-century Christians had it in abundance, enough to die for it. Not because they were naive about the world's capacity for cruelty, but because they were convinced that something had already happened that changed what the cruelty meant.

Is This How the Story Ends?

The world as Solomon described it — wearisome, cyclical, ultimately hollow — is not a place where human beings can generate their own salvation. We have tried. We reduce carbon emissions, and new problems emerge. We build institutions for peace, and they are corrupted. We resolve to be better and find ourselves, by 9 AM, already behind on our own resolutions. The problem is not effort. The problem is that the repair required goes deeper than anything we can reach on our own.

What we need, in the language of this chapter's brutal honesty, is not a better program, or a more inspiring leader, or a more sophisticated philosophy. We need someone who can step into the broken system from outside it — someone not subject to its cycles, not born into its frustration, not carrying the weight of its disconnection — and do something about the cause rather than just the symptoms.

"God is in control," you may have heard Christians say. But if God were in control of this world, the world would not be the way it is. God is in control of heaven — a place where, by every account, things are exactly as they should be. This world is a project gone sideways. And what God chose to do with a project gone sideways was not to scrap it and start over. He chose to climb inside it.

The longing you feel — for a world without injustice, without childhood cancers, without senseless loss, without the grinding repetition of the same old failures — is not a sign that you are naive or sentimental. It is evidence. Evidence that you were designed for something this world was never equipped to give you. And if that is true, then the most important question you can ask is not *why the world is this way*, but *who made me for another one, and where do I find them?*

CHAPTER 3
TO INFINITY AND BEYOND

Here is the problem with God.

Not the theological problem, or the philosophical problem, or the problem of evil — though all of those are real and we will get to them. The most immediate problem with God is a practical one: he does not fit inside the human mind. Not because he is hiding, but because the container is too small. We are finite creatures trying to think clearly about something that exists beyond the outer edge of everything we can measure, imagine, or experience. And when something won't fit in the container we have available, the temptation is to trim it down until it does.

That is exactly what most people do with God. And that is where almost every misunderstanding about him begins.

This chapter is about what God actually looks like when you stop trimming — when you resist the urge to make him manageable and instead try, however imperfectly, to enter his world rather than pulling him down into yours. The math gets strange. The categories stop working the way you expect. But the picture that emerges is far more coherent, far more compelling, and far more useful than the shrunken version most of us were handed.

Fitting Infinity into a Finite World

Buzz Lightyear didn't mean to ask a theological question. But "to infinity and beyond" turns out to be one of the most honest things anyone has said about God — because it points to exactly where our thinking breaks down.

We can handle big. We can handle really, really big. But infinity — something without edges, without beginning, without end — our brains hit a wall. Scientists tell us the universe itself is infinite, that space and time are unbounded. But that pushes the question back a step. Whatever created space and time had to exist outside of them. Which means it wasn't just infinite — it was beyond infinite. Not a bigger version of what we know. Something else entirely.

Consider just how quickly the concept of infinity slips beyond our grasp.

Time, space, and matter form an inseparable continuum — three elements so deeply intertwined that none can exist without the others. If there were matter but no space, where would it exist? If there were matter and space but no time, *when* would it exist? They could not have arrived one at a time. They had to come into being all at once.

What's remarkable is that the Bible captures this in just ten words. *"In the beginning"* — time. *"God created the heaven"* — space. *"And the earth"* — matter. A single sentence, and yet within it, a trinity of trinities: time (past, present, future), space (length, width, height), and matter (solid, liquid, gas) — all bursting into existence simultaneously.

This means they cannot contain the God who created them. Consider a stoplight: the engineer who designed it is not crouched inside the housing, manually flipping the lights from red to green — a programmed system handles that. The designer exists entirely apart from his creation. In the same way, the Creator of this universe is not bound by it. He is above it, beyond it, and woven through it — and yet completely unaffected by it.

That's the problem with God. Not that he's hard to believe in — it's that he's hard to contain. And we really, really want to contain him. We want a God we can predict, explain, and if necessary, argue with. So we do something understandable and completely backwards: we shrink him down to our size. We build a God in our own image — one who thinks like us, reacts like us, and operates by the same logic we use on a Tuesday morning.

And then we hand him lines he never actually said:

- *God has a special plan for your life.*
- *God never gives you more than you can handle.*
- *God is trying to teach you something through this hardship.*
- *God needed another angel in heaven.*
- *It was God's time to take them.*
- *Just let go and let God.*

None of that is in the Bible. Not one line. Those phrases were born in church hallways, on sympathy cards, and in small groups where nobody wanted to sit with a hard question long enough to find an honest answer. They feel comforted for about thirty seconds. Then they collapse — because when the thing they promised doesn't happen, you're not just disappointed. You're done. You walked away from a God who you claim said and did, but never actually said and did.

The atheist's version of this is just as common, and just as human:

- *Why doesn't God just forgive everyone?*
- *How can a loving God let bad things happen to good people?*
- *Why didn't God stop this from happening to me?*
- *Why can't he just make the world right?*
- *Why would a good God send anyone to hell?*

These are real questions. They deserve real engagement, not dismissal. But notice what they all have in common: they assume God should operate the way a reasonable, well-meaning human being would operate. They take a being that exists beyond infinity and measure him against our instincts about fairness, efficiency, and kindness. That's not skepticism. That's still building God in our image — and we've decided he doesn't pass muster.

If that's the God you rejected, I understand completely. I'd reject that God, too.

But here's the move almost nobody tries: instead of pulling God into your world and judging him there, what if you tried stepping into his? Not abandoning your questions — bringing them with you. Not pretending the hard things aren't hard — but being willing to understand him on his terms before rendering a verdict on yours.

That's exactly why Jesus came. Not to send down a doctrinal manual. Not to establish a religion. But to show up in person — to let you see God face to face, in a body, in a specific place and time, dealing with real people and real suffering. He said it plainly: "If you have seen me, you have seen the Father." He is the translation. The beyond infinite, rendered in terms we can actually work with.

You don't have to resolve every question before you take a step toward that. You just have to be willing to look.

You Have Your Moments

You are a mood. Not always — but enough. Happy one hour, irritable the next. Generous on Monday, petty on Wednesday. You snap at people you love, feel terrible about it, and do it again two days later. This is not a character indictment. It's just what it means to be human — to be a creature who lives inside moments, one at a time, riding whatever the current one brings.

God doesn't work that way. Not because he's emotionally flat, but because he doesn't live inside moments at all. He isn't happy right now, but he gets angry later. He isn't forgiving you today and reconsidering tomorrow. He doesn't collect new information about you and update his feelings accordingly. He sees the whole of everything — past, present, future — simultaneously, from outside of time. There is no "right now" for God. Which means there is no mood.

The Greeks and Romans understood that gods were powerful. What they couldn't shake was the suspicion that gods were also, essentially, like them — just bigger and angrier, with better lightning. Zeus had tantrums. Athena held grudges. Mars loved a good war. The entire system of sacrifice and ritual existed for one reason: keep the gods in a good mood, because when they weren't, people died. That was religion as mood management. Exhausting, unstable, and ultimately hopeless — because a god who can be provoked into cruelty is a god you can never fully trust.

We do the same thing today, just with better coffee and worse theology. Listen to what gets said in church hallways, small groups, and sympathy cards, and you'll hear the moody God alive and well:

- *God took her from me.* — God as executioner, pulling people out of your life when he decides it's time.
- *God is trying to teach you something.* — God as cosmic disciplinarian, engineering your suffering for educational purposes.
- *God has a plan for your life.* — God as life coach, with a detailed itinerary he's frustratingly refusing to share.
- *God is causing calamity in your life because you're sinning.* — God as enforcer, sending hardship as an invoice for bad behavior.
- *God wanted me to have this car.* — God as personal shopper, deeply invested in your vehicle preferences.

- *Just let go and let God.* — God as autopilot, waiting for you to stop trying so he can take over.

Not one of these is in the Bible. Not one. Jesus came to show us exactly what God is like — and he never said or did any of these things. Not once. These phrases didn't come from Scripture. They came from people who couldn't sit with uncertainty and needed God to make sense on human terms. So they made him moody. Reactive. A God who punishes, rewards, takes, and gives based on your current standing—a God, in other words, who operates exactly the way we do.

Here's what makes the real God genuinely hard to grasp: he doesn't trade off between emotions. He isn't 50% loving and 50% wrathful, balancing the scales depending on what you did last week. He is 100% just. 100% wrathful. 100% merciful. 100% loving. 100% gracious. All of it, all at once, all the time. If you're doing the math and getting 500%, that's the point. These aren't competing attributes that God cycles through depending on his mood. They are simultaneous, constant, and total. This is not the kind of math that fits inside a finite mind. It wasn't meant to.

What this means practically is that God is not throwing the pitches. He is not the architect of your cancer, your divorce, your bankruptcy, or your dead child. He is not engineering a catastrophe to get your attention or settle a score. The world is doing that — the broken, untethered, spiritually dark world that Chapter 2 described in detail. God didn't build the Hanoi Hilton. He's standing outside it.

With a catcher's mitt.

That image matters more than it might seem. A catcher doesn't throw the ball. He doesn't decide what gets pitched at you, how hard, or where it goes. What he does is position himself to receive whatever comes — ready, steady, eyes open. He is there before the pitch leaves the hand. He is there when it arrives. He doesn't flinch, doesn't step aside, doesn't drop it.

When something in your life goes badly — and something will — the most useful question is not *why did God do this to me?* That question is built on a false premise, and it will take you nowhere good. The question worth asking is: *where is God in this?* The answer, almost always, is the same. Crouched down. Glove up. Already there.

The Embodiment of Justice

Here's a question nobody likes to sit with: if God is 100% loving, why doesn't he forgive everyone and be done with it?

Because forgiveness without justice isn't love, it's corruption.

A judge who lets guilty people walk because he's feeling generous isn't merciful — he's broken. Justice isn't the opposite of love. It's what love looks like when it takes other people seriously. When someone wrongs you, you don't want a God who shrugs. You want a God who sees it. Every victim of every crime, every betrayal, every quiet cruelty that nobody else witnessed — they want justice. And a God who skips it to keep things comfortable isn't a God worth trusting.

So justice is non-negotiable. The question is how it gets applied — and to whom.

Plato wrestled with this in one of the oldest thought experiments on record. In the "Ring of Gyges," a shepherd finds a magic ring that makes him invisible. He uses it to seduce the queen, murder the king, and take the throne. No witnesses. No consequences. No one ever knows. Plato's student Glaucon argued that any rational person would do the same — that human beings are only just when they have to be, when someone is watching. Remove the consequences, and the mask comes off.

He wasn't wrong. We all have a Ring of Gyges. We all have a version of ourselves that only exists in private — the things we do when no one is watching, the thoughts we entertain, the compromises we make when we're sure it won't come up. We present one face to the world and operate differently behind it. The problem isn't that other people can't see it. God can. Every invisible act, every secret negotiation with your own conscience — all of it, fully visible, fully known.

Which brings us to the uncomfortable part.

We are remarkably enthusiastic about justice — right up until it points at us. Think about who you'd put in hell if you were running things. Hitler, obviously. Stalin. The guy down the street, whom you know, is cheating on his wife. Maybe your ex. Probably some politicians. We all have a mental list, and we press those buttons with great satisfaction. In the Austin Powers movies, Dr. Evil has a control panel with a button for each henchman who failed him. He calls their name, presses the button, and they vanish in a puff of smoke. That is exactly how most people imagine divine justice — applied liberally to everyone who deserves it, which is to say, everyone who isn't them.

But here's the thing about a God who is 100% just: he doesn't have a favorites list. He doesn't look the other way for the good guys. He doesn't grade on a curve because you've been mostly decent and your intentions were generally okay. Justice that plays favorites isn't justice — it's just power with better PR. A God who lets Sam off the hook because Sam seems like a good guy, while holding Mary to the standard, is not a just God. He's a corrupt one.

So the button has your name on it. And mine. Alongside Hitler and Stalin and everyone else on your list. The wrath is real, the justice is real, and none of us escapes the accounting on our own.

And then grace walks in and does something that should be impossible.

The same God who is 100% just is simultaneously 100% merciful,

100% loving, 100% gracious—not trading one off against another. All of it, all at once. And what that means — what the entire rest of this book is built on — is that the qualities of wrath and justice write your name on the button, and the qualities of mercy, love, and grace erase it. Not by pretending the wrong didn't happen. Not by lowering the standard. But by absorbing the cost in a way that satisfies justice completely without destroying you.

That's not a loophole. That's the whole point.

The cross isn't God going soft on justice. It's justice fully served, and mercy fully given, at the same time. You don't have to choose between a God who is fair and a God who loves you. In the end, he is furiously, completely, simultaneously both.

Mercy and Grace

People use these words interchangeably. Even experienced Christians do it. They are not the same thing — and the difference matters more than most people realize, because one of them is what keeps you out of the fire, and the other is what God does next.

Mercy is getting let off the hook when you deserve to be on it.

You were doing 50 in a 30. The officer clocked you. He has you dead to rights — speed, time, location, all of it on the radar gun. He walks up to your window, looks at you for a moment, and hands you a warning. No ticket. No points. No insurance spike. You were guilty. The evidence was real. He chose not to use it. That's mercy. It doesn't erase the fact that you were speeding. It just means the penalty wasn't applied.

Mercy is knowable. You can see it coming, ask for it, plead for it. You know what you did, you know what it costs, and you're hoping someone decides to absorb that cost instead of handing it to you. Mercy is the judge who sentences you to time served. Mercy is the creditor who writes off the debt. Mercy is the person you wronged who decides not to make you pay.

Grace is different. Grace doesn't let you off the hook — it acts like the hook was never there.

Grace cannot be asked for. The moment you walk into someone's office and say, "I know I don't deserve this, but..." you've crossed into mercy territory. Grace, by definition, arrives before you knew you needed it, before you had the language to request it, before you even fully understood what was being given. The teacher who bumped your 89 to an A before you ever said a word — that's grace. You didn't earn it. You didn't negotiate for it. It just appeared on your report card.

Here's what makes grace genuinely hard to receive: you can't recognize it until you're convinced you don't deserve it. That's not false modesty — it's the actual mechanism. The person who gossips about a coworker, gets found out, and then shows up at that same coworker's Christmas party expecting a cold shoulder — and instead gets welcomed like a guest of honor — that person experiences something that short-circuits their logic. It doesn't compute. It violates every social contract they know. And that violation, that complete breakdown of what they expected, is exactly what grace feels like from the inside. Disorienting. Unearned. Uncomfortably generous.

Grace also isn't fair — and it's not trying to be. The student who got the A with an 89 didn't earn it. The student with an 88 didn't get it. There's no formula. There's no committee. Someone with the power to give it simply decided to. That offends our sense of fairness because we're always calculating — always keeping score, always tracking who got what relative to what they deserved. Grace ignores that entire ledger. It doesn't resolve the accounting. It tears up the spreadsheet.

And grace must be experienced personally to mean anything. You can explain it all day long in a classroom or a sermon, and it will remain an abstraction — a concept, a doctrine, a word that sounds nice. It only becomes real the moment someone extends it to you directly, when you know with certainty that you didn't deserve what you just received, and they gave it to you anyway. That moment changes something. Not just in your circumstances — in you.

Now put all of that together and point it at God.

You have the Ring of Gyges file — everything you've done in private that nobody saw. God saw it. The justice button has your name on it, and the case is airtight. Mercy says: guilty, penalty not applied. That alone should drop you to your knees.

But God doesn't stop at mercy. He moves to grace.

He doesn't just close the file. He destroys it. He doesn't just decline to punish you — he pursues you. He doesn't wait for you to clean yourself up, find the right words, walk into the right building, or reach some minimum threshold of deserving. He moves first, before you ask, before you knew to ask, before you were even looking in his direction. That is grace operating at full strength — not as a reward for the almost-good-enough, but as a gift to the utterly undeserving.

Mercy keeps you out of the fire. Grace pulls you into the family.

Both are real. Both are his. And neither of them is anything you earned.

Entering God's World of Emotions

The oldest justice system in the world is also the simplest: you hit me, I hit you back. An eye for an eye. A tooth for a tooth. People read that as barbaric, but it was actually a limit — a ceiling on retaliation, not a floor. It said your compensation must match your loss—no more. The punishment fits the crime. Nothing extra for pain and suffering, nothing added for personal satisfaction. Just even. Just square.

Every legal system in the Western world is built on this foundation. Marty punches Sam. Sam has Marty arrested. A court determines the appropriate consequence—the scales balance. Justice is served. We understand this intuitively because we feel it in our bones from childhood — the howl of "that's not fair" is one of the first coherent sentences a child learns to scream. We are wired for reciprocity.

And then Jesus walks in and says: Don't return the punch.

"If anyone slaps you on the right cheek, turn to them the other cheek also."

Before you dismiss that as naïve or spineless, slow down. Because Jesus isn't describing a doormat, he's describing something that requires more discipline, more strength, and more deliberate intention than swinging back ever would.

When I was boxing, I used to spar with a professional fighter who had one rule: he had to absorb everything I threw, but he could only throw me a jab. Nobody in that gym thought he was weak. He was the most controlled person in the room — making a conscious choice, round after round, not to unleash what he was fully capable of. That's not passivity. That's power under discipline. Absorbing a punch and choosing not to return it is one of the hardest things a human being can do. It breaks the cycle. It refuses to let the other person's worst moment dictate your next move. Martin Luther King Jr. said it plainly: "The old law of an eye for an eye leaves everyone blind." He was right. Reciprocal damage doesn't restore anything. It just spreads the wound.

Jesus wasn't introducing a philosophy. He was foreshadowing what he would do himself.

The parable of the Prodigal Son is the clearest picture of it. A son walks up to his father — his living father — and asks for his inheritance early. In the culture of the time, that was the equivalent of saying, "I wish you were dead." Give me what I'd get if you were gone. The father gives it to him. The son takes it, burns through every penny on exactly the kind of living you'd expect, and ends up broke, starving, feeding pigs in a foreign country — the lowest possible place a Jewish man could land. He decides to go home not because he's repentant in any deep sense, but because even his father's servants eat better than this. He rehearses a speech on the walk back. He'll offer to work as a hired hand. He's not expecting the door to be open.

The father sees him coming from a distance. He doesn't wait. He runs.

He doesn't let the son finish the speech. He doesn't say "we need to talk about what you did." He doesn't put him on probation or make him earn his way back. He throws a party: robe, ring, fattened calf — full restoration, nothing withheld, no conditions attached. The son who came home expecting to sleep in the barn is sitting at the head of the table by sundown.

That is mercy opening the door. That is grace throwing the party.

And then there's the older brother. He's been outside working the whole time, faithful, dutiful, and completely furious. He hears the music, finds out what's happening, and refuses to go in. His father comes out and pleads with him. And the older brother unloads:

"All these years I've been slaving for you and never disobeyed your orders. Yet you never gave me even a young goat so I could celebrate with my friends. But when this son of yours who has squandered your property with prostitutes comes home, you kill the fattened calf for him."

He's not wrong about the facts. His brother did squander everything. His brother did blow it spectacularly. His brother does not deserve the party. Every single thing the older brother said is accurate.

And he completely missed the point.

Here's where it gets uncomfortable — because the older brother is alive and well, and he goes to church every Sunday. He's the one who decides who deserves communion and who doesn't. He's the one who makes the gay couple feel like they wandered into the wrong building. He's the one who tracks the sins of the person in the next pew with more diligence than he tracks his own. He has been faithful. He has followed the rules. And the idea that grace lands on people who didn't earn it — people who actively wasted their shot — offends him at a cellular level. The older brother is the reason people who desperately need God stop coming back. He is, in many churches, running the door.

But the father in the story doesn't affirm the older brother's accounting. He doesn't say "you're right, it isn't fair." He says: your brother was dead and is alive. He was lost and is found. That's why we're celebrating.

Grace isn't fair. It was never supposed to be.

Now, here's what the cross actually is — because "Jesus died for your sins" has been repeated so many times, it's lost almost all its force. It's not wrong. It's just incomplete.

When Jesus went to the cross, he was absorbing the punch. Every punch. The full weight of everything that justice required from every human being who ever lived or ever will — he took it. Not because the debt wasn't real. Not because the justice wasn't warranted. But because 100% justice required payment, 100% love refused to let you pay it alone, 100% wrath demanded it be settled fully, 100% mercy had been holding the door open, and 100% grace walked through it and tore up the bill entirely.

The cross isn't just forgiveness. Forgiveness would be mercy — the debt cancelled, the punishment waived. The cross goes further.

It's reconnection. Your soul, which has been floating in spiritual outer space since the moment humanity turned away from God, gets pulled back in — permanently, completely, regardless of what you did or will do—not placed on probation and not given a conditional pass. Restored. Full standing. Ring on the finger, robe on the back, seat at the table.

Your soul was made to be connected to God. That's where it belongs. Everything else in this book is about what happens when that connection holds.

Can You Forget?

This is the hardest thing I'm going to ask you to do in this entire book. Harder than changing your behavior. Harder than admitting you were wrong. Harder, even, than forgiving someone who doesn't deserve it.

I'm asking you to forget what you think you know about God.

Not permanently. Just long enough to look at him without the filter. Because here's the problem: most people who have walked away from God, or who can't take him seriously, or who tried faith and found it hollow — they didn't reject God. They rejected a version of God that God himself would reject. A God with a lightning bolt and a bad temper. A God who takes people before their time and calls it a plan. A God who causes car crashes and cancer to teach you lessons. A God who is keeping score of your failures and will one day settle the account in the worst possible way—a God who is essentially you, but bigger, angrier, and far less forgiving.

Can you set that down for a moment? Can you put it on a shelf, walk away, and look at what's actually there?

Because if you can, here's what shifts: you stop asking why God did this to you, and you start seeing it clearly — the world did this to you. Not God. The world.

Picture a highway. Multiple lanes, high speed, everyone assuming the cars around them are under control. Then one vehicle loses it — spins out, crosses lanes, hits the median, bounces back into traffic. It doesn't choose its targets. It doesn't discriminate. It just takes out whatever is in its path — indiscriminately, mechanically, without malice or meaning. That's the world. That's what Chapter 2 was describing. A runaway vehicle that has been loose on the highway since the moment humanity broke its connection with God, leaving a trail of broken bones, shattered families, and unanswered prayers in its wake. God didn't send the car into your lane. But you got hit anyway. Everyone does eventually.

The question is whether you have something to hold onto when it happens.

Here's where most people get it backwards. They take the damage the world did to them, hold it up to God, and say, "explain yourself." They put God in the defendant's chair and expect him to answer for every crash, every loss, every prayer that seemed to go nowhere. And when his answers don't satisfy — when they feel like platitudes or silence — they conclude that he's either absent, indifferent, or fictional.

But that's still fitting God into your world. That's still measuring an infinite being by the logic of a finite one. It's still the same mistake, just dressed up as skepticism.

What if you tried the other direction? What if instead of dragging God into your framework and judging him there, you stepped — even tentatively, even suspiciously — into his? Not abandoning your questions. Not pretending the pain wasn't real. But being willing to understand him on his terms before rendering a verdict on yours.

That single shift changes everything. Not because the hard things stop being hard. But because you stop experiencing them as evidence that God failed you, and start seeing them as the predictable damage of a broken world that God is actively working to restore. You are not the victim of a divine plan that included your suffering. You are a soul navigating a wrecked highway, and someone is standing at the exit with a catcher's mitt, waiting.

This whole chapter has been building to one thing. Infinity you can't contain. Math that doesn't add up. Grace, that isn't fair. A God who is simultaneously everything at once, all the time, without contradiction. It's genuinely hard to hold.

But here's the thing — it would be a lot easier if God just came down here, put on a body, walked around in the mess with us, and showed us exactly who he is.

He did.

CHAPTER 4
IN (PEOPLE, PLACES, AND THINGS) WE TRUST

"We can get through this thing all right. We have to stick together; we have to have faith in each other."
-George Bailey from "It's a Wonderful Life"
after there was a run on his bank.

Faith has a reputation problem.

Most people hear the word and immediately think of religion — of pews and creeds and belief in things that cannot be proven. And because of that association, a lot of people who would not describe themselves as religious assume that faith is something they do not practice. Something for other people. Something that requires a particular kind of credulity they were not born with.

They are wrong. And this chapter is about why.

Faith is not a religious category. It is a human one. You use it constantly, automatically, without thinking about it — and you could not function for a single day without it. Once you understand that, the question of whether to have faith in God stops being a question about whether you are the kind of person who believes in things you cannot see. Because you already are. The only question is what you are pointing that faith toward.

Faith Every Day

You already have faith. You've had it your whole life. You don't call it that.

Every time you sit in a chair without checking the welds, you're exercising faith. Every time you schedule surgery and show up at 8 AM, assuming the surgeon will too, that's faith. Every time you deposit a paycheck and trust it'll be there when you need it, it's faith. You are not a skeptic living in a world of certainties. You are a person navigating constant uncertainty, placing trust in things you cannot fully verify, dozens of times a day, without breaking a sweat.

Faith is not the opposite of reason. It's what reason does when it runs out of certainty, which is most of the time. The line between what you know and what you're betting on is a lot blurrier than most people want to admit.

Here's where it gets interesting. The people most likely to dismiss religious faith as irrational are often the same people who have placed enormous faith in science, which is not the same thing as fact. "Scientists say" is not a guarantee. It's a current best estimate, subject to revision. In the 1970s, scientists said carbon emissions were cooling the planet toward a new ice age. The same mechanism — carbon — is now warming it. Both positions required the public to trust conclusions they couldn't personally verify. That's faith operating inside a lab coat.

Put it side by side, and it looks like this:

The believer says: God created life, the stars, the universe. I trust that's true. I have hope and confidence in it, even though I wasn't there and I can't replicate it in a controlled environment.

The atheist says: The Big Bang created everything. Natural selection produced all life on Earth. I trust that's true. I have confidence in it, even though no one has witnessed the Big Bang, no one has observed one species become another in real time, and life has never been created in a laboratory from non-living matter.

Both positions require you to trust something you cannot personally verify. Both require a leap. The difference is not faith versus no faith. The difference is what — or who — you're placing your faith in.

And that question matters more than most people want to sit with. Because faith isn't neutral, it moves in a direction. It shapes outcomes. The more evidence you accumulate about something — good reports, reliable track record, consistent performance — the more your faith grows. The more it fails you, the more it erodes. You've experienced this. A doctor who's been wrong twice loses your confidence the third time around. A hospital with a bad reputation doesn't get your trust just because it asks for it.

Jesus understood this. He never asked for blind faith — a leap into darkness with no basis for the jump. He asked for faith built on evidence. Look at what he did. Look at who he was. Look at what happened after. Then decide. Faith in him isn't a religious requirement designed to keep you in line. It's an invitation to place your trust in something with an extraordinary track record—and see what kinds of outcomes follow.

Faith plus evidence produces hope. And hope, as Chapter 2 described, is the one thing this world is structurally incapable of providing on its own.

Trust Every Day

Trust is not a feeling. It's a track record.

You don't trust your bank because it seems nice. You trust it because it has returned your money every time you've asked for it. You don't trust a surgeon because he has a good handshake. You trust him because his patients come out the other side. Trust is built from evidence, accumulated over time, tested under pressure. It is the most rational thing in the world — and the most fragile.

You already know how this works in relationships, because you've felt it break. Marriage runs on trust. The moment one spouse suspects the other isn't where they said they were, something shifts — not just in the relationship, but in the body. The stomach drops. The mind starts running scenarios. That physical response is your entire trust architecture going into emergency mode, because trust isn't just emotional. It's structural. It holds things up. When it goes, everything built on top of it goes with it.

The same is true between parents and children, between business partners, and between friends who've known each other for twenty years. Trust grows through time spent together, through showing up, through doing what you said you would do when it would have been easier not to. The longer that pattern holds, the deeper the confidence goes — until you reach the point where you don't have to think about it anymore. You know. And when that pattern breaks, the damage is rarely proportional. A single betrayal can erase years of reliability. That's not irrational. That's how trust actually works.

It's also exactly how trust in God works — and exactly how it breaks down.

Here's the connection that most people miss. Trust and faith are not the same thing, but they move together. The more you trust someone, the more certain you become about future outcomes with them. That certainty is faith — not blind faith, but evidence-based confidence built from a history of showing up. Your bank doesn't ask you to believe in it blindly. It shows you a track record and asks you to extend that pattern forward. Jesus operates on the same logic. He doesn't ask you to leap into darkness. He points to what he did, what he said, what happened after — and asks whether that track record is worth trusting.

But here's where it gets personal. Because some of you didn't leave God casually. You left because you trusted him with something that mattered — really mattered — and the outcome wasn't what you prayed for. You brought him your marriage, your child, your health, your desperate 3 AM prayer, and the answer you got back felt like silence. Or worse, like a no. And when that happened, the trust took a hit. Not a small one. The kind that makes you reluctant to go back, because going back means risking it again, and you're not sure you can take another loss like the last one.

That's not a weakness. That's an honest response to a real experience. And it deserves a real answer — not a platitude, not a bumper sticker about God's mysterious ways.

Here it is: trust in God was never meant to be a transaction. It was never a vending machine where prayer goes in, and miracles come out. The original breakdown between humanity and God — the one Chapter 1 described — happened precisely because we decided the relationship was transactional. We suspected God was holding out on us, that the connection was more for his benefit than ours. We stopped trusting him and went our own way. And the world has been dealing with the fallout ever since.

What God has been doing — through everything, including the silence, including the unanswered prayers, including the outcomes that made no sense — is working to restore what broke. Not by eliminating the hardship. Not by guaranteeing that every prayer lands the way you hoped. But by being the one constant that doesn't move, doesn't waver, and doesn't stop reaching — even when you've stopped looking.

The question isn't whether God failed your trust. The question is whether you were trusting the right version of him in the first place. Because a God who promises to give you everything you ask for, on your timeline, with outcomes you approve of — that God doesn't exist. But a God who absorbs the worst the world can throw, who takes the punch so you don't have to, who restores full standing to people who burned every bridge they had, and promises a guaranteed outcome — that God has an extraordinary track record.

And track records are exactly what trust is built on.

Your Faith Lens

You don't see the world as it is. You see it as you are — filtered through every experience that ever taught you who to trust, what to fear, and what to expect from people when things get hard.

That filter is your faith lens. And it was built without your permission, starting before you were old enough to know.

Your parents' marriage — or the absence of one — taught you something about commitment before you had a word for it. The teacher who humiliated you in front of the class taught you something about authority. The friend who told your secret taught you something about vulnerability. The parent who left, the one who stayed but shouldn't have, the one who was there physically but somewhere else entirely — all of it went in. All of it became data. And your developing mind did exactly what it was designed to do: it found the pattern, drew the conclusion, and built a lens to match.

Happy childhoods produce people who extend trust relatively easily, who assume good intent, who walk into rooms without scanning for exits. Damaged childhoods produce something different — people who are always slightly braced, who read situations for threat before they read them for opportunity, who mistake wariness for wisdom because wariness kept them safe when they needed it most.

The problem is that a lens built for survival in one environment doesn't automatically recalibrate when the environment changes. You carry it with you. Into your marriage. Into your friendships. Into your relationship with God. The person who learned early that the people who were supposed to protect them didn't — that person doesn't suddenly trust easily just because the situation is different now. The wound doesn't heal. It just goes underground and starts making decisions from there.

This is what PTSD actually looks like from the inside — and it's worth naming clearly, because too many people carry it without knowing what to call it. PTSD isn't just for combat veterans. It's the residue of any experience that overwhelmed your ability to process it at the time. It makes you feel permanently on guard, scanning for danger that may not be there, numb to the people trying to get close, overprotective of the ones you love in ways that push them away. Intimacy becomes a threat assessment. Vulnerability becomes a liability. The nervous system that was once trying to keep you alive is now running the same emergency protocols in situations that don't require them — and you can't just decide to turn it off.

That kind of damage doesn't just affect how you relate to people. It goes all the way down to how you relate to God. Because if the people who were supposed to love you unconditionally came with conditions, why would God be different? If trust has always eventually been broken, why extend it to someone you can't even see? The faith lens that the world and your history built doesn't leave room for a God who is 100% loving, 100% consistent, and incapable of changing his mind about you. That sounds like a sales pitch. And you've heard sales pitches before.

Here's the hard truth: the lens you're looking through right now was largely constructed by a world that, as Chapter 2 described, is not on your side. It was shaped by pain that was done to you, by betrayals you didn't deserve, by systems and people that failed you in ways that left marks. And now you're using that lens to evaluate everything — including whether God is real, whether he's trustworthy, whether any of this is worth your time.

That's not a moral failing. It's physics. You can only see through the lens you have.

But here's what matters: a lens can be recalibrated. It isn't permanent. The corruption isn't the final word on what you're capable of seeing. The process is slow, and it's real work, and it doesn't happen by white-knuckling your way to a better attitude. It happens gradually, incrementally, exposing the lens to something that contradicts what it was built to expect — something that shows up consistently, tells the truth, and doesn't flinch when you test it.

That's exactly what the next section is about.

Leaving Your Religion Behind

This is going to bother some people. Good.

If your religion is getting in the way of Jesus, leave it behind. Not Jesus — your religion. The rituals nobody explained—the rules somebody made up. The theology stitched together from three different Bible passages that don't belong in the same sentence. The God who was presented to you as part bouncer, part genie, part disappointed parent. Leave all of it because Jesus didn't come to start a religion. He came to fix a broken connection. And an enormous amount of what gets called Christianity today is noise between you and that signal.

When Jesus showed up, he didn't validate the religious

establishment of his time. He dismantled it. The Pharisees had built an elaborate system of rules, rituals, and interpretations layered on top of what God actually said — and Jesus called it out, publicly, repeatedly, without apology. He wasn't anti-God. He was anti-religion-as-performance. He was against anything that put distance between a human soul and the God that soul was built to connect with. That hasn't changed. The packaging is different today — different denominations, different buildings, different coffee shops in the lobby — but the same disease runs through it. Rituals that nobody can explain. Doctrines assembled from Old Testament passages yanked out of context and fused with something from Paul's letters to produce a commandment God never issued. Faith healing. Prosperity gospel. Communion withheld as punishment. Saints prayed to—purple cloths on statues. If you can't find it in the words of Jesus, be very suspicious of anyone who tells you that God requires it.

Jesus said two things: believe in me, and follow me. That's the whole assignment. Everything else is someone else's agenda wearing a clerical collar.

Now — the hypocrites. Let's talk about them, because they may be the real reason you're reading this with your arms crossed.

The pastor who preached on Sunday was caught on Wednesday. The church that welcomed you warmly until they found out who you voted for, who you loved, or what you'd done. The Christians down the street who were holy rollers at the 10 AM service and something else entirely by Saturday night. The church lady who told you, with complete confidence, that you were going to hell for being exactly who you are. The community that was supposed to be a shelter turned out to be just another place where you didn't measure up.

I'm not going to tell you those experiences weren't real. They were real. The damage was real. And the people who caused it will have to account for it. But here's what I need you to see: they were not Jesus. Not even close. They were people with their own corrupted faith lenses, their own unresolved damage, their own institutional incentives — using Jesus' name as a credential while doing things he never sanctioned and saying things he never said. Don't hand them the power to define him. Don't let the fraud determine your verdict on the real thing. You wouldn't swear off medicine because a bad doctor hurt you. Don't swear off Jesus because bad Christians failed you.

And don't walk away because right-wing political operatives have weaponized the Bible to push an agenda Jesus would find unrecognizable. Don't walk away because someone told you God made promises he never made — that good behavior earns good outcomes, that faith is a hedge against suffering, that the righteous get the good parking spots. None of that is the gospel. It's a distortion of it, and it has done incalculable damage to people who deserved better.

Here's what Jesus actually offers. Not a better set of rules. Not a religious identity. Not a political tribe. A different lens entirely.

The lens you have right now — the one built from everything that happened to you, everything that was done to you, everything you watched fall apart — that lens sees this world on its own terms. It measures God by human standards and finds him wanting. It looks at suffering and concludes that there is an absence. It examines unanswered prayer and concludes with indifference. That's not stupidity. That's a damaged lens doing exactly what damaged lenses do.

Jesus offers to replace it. Not overnight. Not by erasing your history. But gradually, as trust builds, as the track record accumulates, as you begin to see your circumstances — the doctor's call, the job loss, the marriage that didn't survive — through the eyes of someone who exists outside of time and sees the whole story, not just the chapter you're stuck in right now.

Paul, writing to the church in Rome, put the foundation of this in one sentence: *"While we were still sinners, Christ died for us."* Not after we cleaned up. Not after we found the right church, said the right prayer, or figured out the right way to believe. While we were still a mess. That's when he moved. That's the promise the cross actually makes — not that life will get easier, but that the connection is restored, permanently, unconditionally, regardless of what your faith lens currently tells you about whether you deserve it.

You don't have to have it all figured out. You don't have to resolve every question, forgive every hypocrite, or untangle every piece of religious baggage before you take a step. You just have to be willing to look through a different lens for a moment.

Jesus said it simply: *"Come to me, all you who are weary and burdened, and I will give you rest."*

Not the church. Not the religion. Not the institution. Him. Following him is key to getting a new faith lens. The rest of this book is devoted to reshaping your lens. The invitation to reshape it is still open. It has your name on it. And it doesn't expire.

CHAPTER 5
ERASURE POETRY

"Erasure poetry, also known as blackout poetry, is a form of found poetry wherein a poet takes an existing text and erases, blacks out, or otherwise obscures a large portion of the text, creating a wholly new work from what remains." Poets.org

There are two weights most people carry through life without ever putting them down.

The first is what someone did to you — the injury, the betrayal, the thing that was taken and never given back, the apology that never came. You have been waiting for that apology, perhaps for years. It has not arrived. And in its absence, something has hardened.

The second is what you did. The thing you cannot undo. The version of yourself from ten years ago, or twenty, or last Tuesday, that you would give almost anything to revise. You have not forgotten it. You are not sure you are allowed to.

This chapter is about both of those weights — where they come from, what they do to you, and what it looks like when they are finally set down. The title is deliberate. Erasure is exactly what is on offer.

Not a reduced sentence. Not a payment plan. Not a grudging pardon issued from a distance. Erasure. As if it never happened.

That is a large claim. Let's build up to it honestly.

Debtor Poetry

Debt Transactions

Think about the last time you carried a balance on your credit card. Even if you pay it off every month, that debt exists from the moment you swipe until the moment the payment clears. It doesn't disappear on its own. Someone has to settle it. That's how debt works — it doesn't vanish, it gets paid.

The same principle runs through every relationship you have.

When someone hurts you, something real is taken from you. Your spouse makes a cutting remark about the dishes, and what's lost is not just a moment — it's a piece of your dignity. A colleague takes credit for your work, and what's gone is your sense of recognition. A friend betrays your confidence, and trust walks out the door. Divorce strips away the family you built. Gossip quietly steals your reputation. In each case, the person who hurt you now owes you something, and we all know intuitively what that something is: an apology. That's where the phrase comes from — "you owe me an apology." It isn't just an expression. It's an accurate description of what happened.

This is the debt-debtor relationship, and it shows up everywhere. Just like financial debt, it doesn't resolve itself. The account stays open until something is done about it.

Here's where it gets complicated. Most of the time, the apology never comes. And so the debt just sits there, accumulating interest in the form of resentment, replayed conversations, and quiet anger. The person who hurt you may not even know the account is still open. But you do.

What you do with that open account — that's what the rest of this chapter is about

Missing Apology

Here's what happens after you've been hurt and the person who did it hasn't said a word. You wait. Not always consciously — sometimes it's just a low hum in the background of your day. But the account is open, the debt is real, and somewhere in the back of your mind, you're keeping the books.

While you wait, your imagination gets to work. You begin rehearsing a scene that hasn't happened yet — and may never happen. In it, the person who hurt you finally comes around. Maybe they call, voice cracking with regret. Maybe it happens at the office, in front of the same colleagues who witnessed the original offense. Your spouse, who once dismissed you in front of the kids, sits across from you with tears in their eyes and says, "You were right. I'm sorry. I'll do better." The friend who spread rumors about you gets cornered by the truth and has no choice but to apologize publicly. In every version of the fantasy, you are vindicated. They are diminished—justice, at last.

It's a satisfying scene — while it lasts. The problem is, you keep coming back to reality, and nothing has changed. The apology hasn't come. So the fantasy sharpens. Now it's not just an apology, it's a reckoning. You don't just want them to say sorry — you want them to understand the full weight of what they did. You want them to feel it. And in your mind, they do. You say exactly what you've always wanted to say, and for once, they have no comeback.

Eventually, you bring it to the people around you. A close friend, a sibling, maybe a coworker who witnessed the whole thing. You lay it out — what happened, how unfair it was, how you've been wronged.

And they listen. They nod. They say the right things. But after a while — sometimes gently, sometimes not so gently — they say the thing you were hoping to avoid: "You need to let this go."

Which is infuriating. Because letting it go feels like surrender. It feels like you're doing them a favor they haven't earned. Why should you be the one to release the debt? They're the one who owes it.

So instead, you do what most people do. You stuff it. You tell yourself you're fine, that you've moved on, that it doesn't really bother you anymore. You pack the hurt into an imaginary bag and tie it shut. Life continues. Work, family, routines — all of it keeps moving.

But the bag doesn't disappear. It rides along with you. And the longer the apology doesn't come, the heavier it gets — stuffed with not just the original hurt, but every reminder of it, every moment the wound got bumped, every time you had to act like everything was fine when it wasn't. You carry it to the dinner table. You carry it into new friendships. You carry it into the next relationship, already braced for betrayal.

What starts as hurt quietly hardens into anger. And when anger has nowhere to go, it turns inward — into a low-grade depression that's hard to name and even harder to shake. You're not sad, exactly. You're just tired. Tired of carrying something you never asked to carry, waiting for a resolution that never seems to come.

I understand the reluctance to forgive. I genuinely do. Whatever happened to you — I'm not dismissing it. Some of the debts people carry are enormous: a parent who was never there, a spouse who walked out, a betrayal that cost you everything. These aren't small things. And the idea that you should simply forgive and move on can feel like being asked to pretend the wrong never happened.

But here's what refusing to forgive actually does to you. That's where we're going next.

The Deadly Refusal

Refusing to forgive feels righteous. That's what makes it so dangerous.

From the inside, holding onto the hurt makes complete sense. You were wronged. The debt is real. The other person hasn't paid it. So you hold the account open — not out of weakness, but out of a perfectly reasonable sense of justice. What you may not realize is that the refusal to forgive isn't hurting them. It's hurting you.

Science has caught up with what Scripture has said for centuries. Researchers at Johns Hopkins found that people who hold onto grudges are significantly more likely to experience severe depression and post-traumatic stress disorder, along with a range of other serious health conditions. This isn't abstract. The anger you are carrying is doing something to you — to your sleep, your blood pressure, your immune system, your ability to be present in your own life.

And it doesn't stay contained. That dirty laundry bag you've been stuffing? It starts to spill over.

It spills into your friendships. You're quicker to take offense now, quicker to assume the worst. A friend says something offhand, and you hear something pointed. A colleague disagrees with you, and suddenly it feels personal. People who love you start to feel like they're walking on eggshells, and they can't quite explain why.

It spills into your marriage. The anger that started with one person bleeds into the relationship you go home to every night. Your spouse didn't cause this wound, but they're living with it. Small disagreements carry more weight than they should. The emotional distance grows — quietly, incrementally — until one day you both realize you've been living like roommates for months.

It follows you to work. You become harder to deal with, quicker to assume that people are out to get you, because that's what happened before, and you will not be caught off guard again. Opportunities for new relationships — friendships, mentorships, collaborations — start to feel risky. So you keep your distance. And the isolation deepens.

Here is what the refusal to forgive ultimately costs you: it costs you the present. The person who hurt you has moved on — or worse, they don't even know you're still carrying this. Meanwhile, you are still in that moment, still waiting for a resolution that may never come, still organized around a debt that was never going to be paid the way you needed it to be.

You wrapped their offense around your ankle and called it justice. But it isn't justice. It's a chain. And you are the only one wearing it.

God Feels the Same Way

Before you dismiss this idea, sit with it for a moment. Everything we've been talking about — the hurt, the open account, the waiting, the anger when nothing gets paid back — God knows that experience from the inside, not as a distant observer. As someone who has been on the receiving end of it, repeatedly, from the people he loves most.

Think about what gets taken from him.

Every time you put something else at the center of your life — your career, your bank account, your reputation — you've bumped God out of first place. That's not a small thing to him. Every time you treat someone poorly because of the color of their skin, their background, or who they love, you are mocking something he made and called good. Every time you take the gifts he wired into you and waste them chasing more — more money, more status, more of whatever your neighbor has — that's a slap in the face to the one who gave you those gifts in the first place.

And it goes further. When you go through a whole day — or a whole year — without talking to him, without acknowledging that he's there, you've essentially told him he doesn't matter. When you use his name as punctuation for your frustration and never give it another thought, you've reduced him to a curse word. When you stood at an altar and made a promise before him, only to break it, you handed him another open account. When you've been vindictive toward someone who may not even deserve it, you've taken his sense of justice and trampled it.

The list is long. And if you are honest with yourself, you already know most of what's on it.

Now here is where the parallel gets uncomfortably close. Remember what you felt when the apology never came? Remember the justified anger, the sense that something real had been taken and never returned? God feels the weight of that, too. He is not a distant, unmoved force watching human behavior with indifference. He is a spirit, but also like a person, and people feel the sting of being dismissed, disrespected, and abandoned by the ones they love.

The difference is what he does with it.

You waited for an apology that never came, and the hurt calcified into resentment. God looked at the same open accounts — every one of them, across every person who ever lived — and instead of waiting, he acted. Not with punishment, not with the cold shoulder, not with the quiet withdrawal that most of us reach for when we've been hurt enough times. He sent his son to settle every debt that was ever owed to him. Not because it was deserved. Not because the apology finally came. But because he decided that the relationship mattered more than the balance sheet.

That is not a small thing. That is the most radical act of forgiveness in human history — and it was directed at you, specifically, for the full list of everything you've taken from him. Every single item, cancelled.

Which makes it worth asking: if that is how God responded to your debt, what does he have a right to expect from you when it comes to the debts others owe you?

God Won't Lower His Standards

Let's be honest about something. When we're in pain, when the weight of our own failures or someone else's is pressing down hard, most of us secretly wish God would just look the other way. Lower the bar a little. Make an exception. Surely, given everything, he could find it in himself to be a little more flexible.

He won't. And if you think about it carefully, you wouldn't actually want him to.

A God who bends his standards based on circumstances isn't a God you can trust. He's a variable — shifting with the wind, adjusting his expectations based on who's asking and how badly they need a break. That kind of God offers no real anchor. You'd never know where you stood. The very thing that makes God reliable — the thing that makes him worth orienting your life around — is that he doesn't change. His nature is fixed. His standard of righteousness is absolute. And that standard requires that every debt be fully accounted for.

This is not cruelty. It's justice. And deep down, you believe in it too.

Think about the last time someone wronged you badly — really badly. Cheated you out of something significant, betrayed your trust in a way that cost you dearly. Did you want God to shrug and let it go? Did you want the universe to simply absorb it and move on? Of course not. You wanted it to matter. You wanted there to be a reckoning. That instinct for justice isn't a character flaw — it's a reflection of the God who made you. He wired that into you because it reflects something true about his own nature.

The problem is that the same standard you want applied to the people who wronged you also applies to you. Every debt you've accumulated falls under the same requirement. One hundred percent justice. No exceptions, no sliding scale, no partial credit for good intentions.

So how does anyone get out from under that?

This is precisely where Jesus enters. Not to lower the standard — but to meet it, completely, on your behalf. And the way he does it follows the same logic as the forgiveness he asks of you.

That's because Jesus showed us that forgiveness is not a series of lip-service words; it's a process, a set of actions, a conscious decision, where no apology is required from the offending person because, as we know, the apology may never come. The picture that Jesus paints of forgiveness is the same as cancelling a debt:

1. First, identify what was taken from you: a marriage, a childhood, a friendship, trust, respect, etc.
2. Then say to yourself, "That debt is hereby cancelled."
3. Repeat this every time you think of that debt.
4. Then you refuse any payment on that debt.

This is the exact mechanism that God uses when he forgives your debt. His process is a little different because he requires 100% justice. In a way, you can say that God has his judicial system:

1. God identifies what has been taken from him.
2. He then looks at the cross, which in totality is the 100% requirement for justice because the cross is the 100% requirement for wrath.
3. He then uses 100% mercy and 100% forgiveness to reconnect your soul to him.

4. He will never bring up the debt again or hold it against you.

No Regrets

It's step four that stops people in their tracks. God will never bring the debt up again. Not when things go sideways in your life, not when you die, not ever. The ledger is closed. Some people have been told otherwise — that God is keeping score, waiting for the right moment to call it in. He isn't. When God cancels a debt, it stays cancelled.

You are free to go. But understand what that means and what it doesn't. Cancelling the debt doesn't mean the world forgets it. Other people in your life — society, your relationships, the people you hurt — they run their own collections departments, and God doesn't manage those for you. It also doesn't mean you are required to reconcile with the person who hurt you or the person you hurt. In cases of abuse, separation is not only acceptable — it's the right call. Sometimes the right outcome is simply a new set of boundaries with a family member, or an honest acknowledgment that you and another person no longer belong in each other's lives. In marriage, reconciliation may still be worth pursuing — but that's a separate conversation. The point here is that the debt between you and God has been resolved. Full stop.

Here is what makes Christianity unlike anything else on the religious landscape: it is the only faith tradition in which the deity himself absorbs the debt. Every other system puts the burden on you — animal sacrifices, burnt offerings, elaborate rituals designed to appease an offended God. The assumption is always the same: you owe, so you pay. But Jesus flips the entire transaction. Instead of demanding payment, He steps in as the payment. He takes the debt onto himself and cancels it. No other religion on earth offers this. Not one.

And yet, despite this being the entire engine of the faith, you'd never know it watching a lot of Christians operate. They are quick to want their own debts cancelled and slow — painfully slow — to cancel anyone else's. The French author La Rochefoucauld once said that hypocrisy is the tribute vice pays to virtue. That's exactly what's happening when someone wears the WWJD bracelet, carries their Bible under their arm, and still refuses to cancel the debts of addicts, convicts, or people whose lives look different from theirs. Their contempt pays lip service to the very cross that cleared their account. That's not a minor inconsistency — that's the whole thing turned upside down.

The cross is not a limited resource. It does not run dry, does not file for bankruptcy, and does not cap out after a certain number of cancelled debts. God's capacity to clear the account is total and permanent. The moment you look at your situation through the lens of Jesus, you are not disconnected from him — not even close.

This is why I don't approach God as though I owe him a running tally of apologies. The debt is gone. That means I don't need to perform payments — and neither do you. In certain churches, confession has been reduced to a transaction: say the right words, repeat the right prayers, and the account resets until next time. But that's not in the New Testament. Nowhere. Payment was never requested because it was never required. Treating it as required suggests the cross wasn't enough. It was.

What God does ask is this: because your debt has been cancelled, go and cancel the debts of others. Not because they deserve it, not because they apologized, not because reconciliation is guaranteed — but because that is how the mechanism works. You cannot shrug your shoulders and say "let it go" without actually doing the work of letting it go. God didn't shrug at your debt. He dealt with it through a deliberate, costly process. He expects the same from you — not lip service, but a conscious, repeated decision to stop collecting on what you are owed. Pray about the fallout: the anger, the broken relationships, the lost family members. Ask God to help you find a way through it, and if reconciliation is ever possible, to help you find that too.

Clearing your debt is not the finish line. It's the starting line. Too often, "Jesus died for our sins" gets preached as though it's the whole story — as though the point of the cross was simply to zero out the balance and send you on your way. That's not wrong, but it is wildly incomplete. A life lived disconnected from God is a life spent looking at the world through the wrong lens — missing the clarity, purpose, and satisfaction that come from being properly aligned with the one who created you. The cancelled debt opens the door. What you do with the open door is where the real story begins. Forgiveness — yours for others, God's for you — is not the destination. It is the beginning of rest for the soul.

Guilt Poetry

Guilt Complex

Guilt is the thing you can't quite put down. It might be something you did years ago that still surfaces at odd moments — in the quiet of a long drive, in the middle of an otherwise ordinary Tuesday. It might be something you're doing right now, in secret, that you haven't told anyone about. It might not even be something you chose — a decision you made under impossible circumstances, where someone got hurt no matter which way you turned. However it got there, it's there. And it has a weight to it that most of us underestimate.

Guilt and shame are often used interchangeably, but they're not the same thing. Shame is public — it's the exposure of something in front of others. Guilt is more personal, more interior. It lives in the private spaces of your life, in the things you know only you know.

For our purposes here, we'll use guilt to cover both the private burden and the public one.

Left unexamined, guilt doesn't stay put. It spreads.

Psychologist Kendra Cherry describes what she calls a "guilt complex" — a persistent, chronic belief that you have done something wrong, or that you are about to. It doesn't just make you feel bad in the moment; it reshapes the way you see yourself over time. You begin to believe, somewhere beneath the surface, that you don't deserve good things. That happiness is for other people. That if anyone really knew you — the full version, not the edited one you present to the world — they would think far less of you. So you manage the distance carefully. You keep people at arm's length. You become very skilled at controlling what others see.

And then the narratives start. You know the ones. They run on a loop, usually late at night or in unguarded moments:

- "I can't believe I did that to my children."
- "It wasn't just me — there were other factors, other people involved."
- "I was so young. What did I know?"
- "His mother didn't help either."
- "I couldn't escape the way I was raised."

These aren't just excuses — they're survival mechanisms. The mind reaches for anything that softens the weight a little, that distributes the blame more evenly, that makes the thing you did feel less entirely yours. And sometimes there's even truth in them. But the loop itself — the repetition, the rehearsal, the constant returning to the scene — that's not processing. That's carrying.

Here is what unexamined guilt quietly does to a person. It makes you hard to be around in ways that are difficult to trace back to the source. You become the overprotective parent who can't explain why they hover. Or the permissive one who can't hold a boundary because boundaries feel like punishment, and you've already done enough damage. You become the person in relationships who is either too aggressive or too withdrawn — overcorrecting in one direction or the other because the middle ground, where you'd have to be simply present and honest, feels too exposed. You become quick to find fault in others and slow to acknowledge your own — not because you're arrogant, but because you've buried the guilt so deep that it has quietly turned into anger, and anger always needs somewhere to point.

And underneath all of it, the depression. Not always the kind that announces itself — sometimes it's just a flatness, a low ceiling on your days, a sense that something essential is missing and you can't quite name it. You're functioning. You're showing up. But you're not really there.

Here is why we don't just face it and be done with it. Facing guilt head-on means standing in front of something you can't undo. You cannot go back and be the parent your child needed in those early years. You cannot unsay what was said in that argument, or undo what happened on that trip, or return a marriage to what it was before. The past is fixed. And staring directly at something fixed and painful, with no ability to change it, feels unbearable. So we don't. We look slightly to the side of it. We keep moving. We tell ourselves it's behind us, even when we can feel it right there, just over our shoulder.

But here's the thing about guilt that never gets addressed: it doesn't stay behind you. It walks with you. Into every new relationship, every new beginning, every room you enter, trying to be someone slightly different from the person who did that thing. You can't outrun your own story. It was never meant to be left behind.

The question is what you do with it from here.

A Weird Place

Here is the good news. And it is genuinely good.

You do not have to invent a narrative to survive your past. You do not have to keep rewriting the story so that you come out looking better than you did. You do not have to spend the rest of your life either dragging your guilt behind you or running from it. There is another option — and it changes everything.

The cross did more than forgive your sins. That is the part most people hear about, and it is true, and it matters enormously. But the cross also carried your guilt and your shame. All of it. The thing you did on that business trip. The way you parented in those early years when you didn't know what you were doing, and the children paid for it. The marriage you couldn't hold together. The secret you've never told anyone. The version of yourself you'd be mortified for people to see. The cross took all of that — not just the legal record of it, but the weight of it.

The Apostle Paul understood this from the inside, and his story is worth sitting with. Before his encounter with Jesus on the road to Damascus, Paul had spent years hunting down followers of Jesus and having them imprisoned and executed. These weren't abstract enemies to him — they were real people, with families, with mothers who grieved them. After his conversion, Paul had to return to those same communities. He had to look people in the eye who had lost someone because of him. He had to preach grace to people who had every reason to spit at his feet.

How do you carry that? How do you stand up and speak about the love of God when you know what you did?

Paul wrestled with it. He called himself the worst of sinners — not as false modesty, but as a clear-eyed acknowledgment of what he had done. And then, after wrestling with it long enough, he landed somewhere remarkable. He wrote, simply and without qualification: "There is no condemnation in Christ Jesus." Not "there is reduced condemnation" or "there is condemnation for most things but not this." No condemnation. Full stop.

That is the weird place. It is the place where your past is neither forgotten nor condemned. You can look at it clearly — study it, even — without being destroyed by it. You carry the memory but not the sentence. You live with the knowledge of what you did without being defined by it. The guilt is real. The shame was real. And yet you are not condemned.

This is, admittedly, a strange place to inhabit. Most people on either side of you won't understand it. Those who don't know Jesus will watch you carry your past without being crushed by it and assume you must not really grasp what you did — that you're in denial, that you haven't truly reckoned with it. And some Christians, frankly, will make the same assumption. The idea that someone can be fully guilty and fully free at the same time doesn't compute in a world that runs on ledgers. Maybe it's because the only alternative that the world has when you do something despicable is to condemn you – it can't save you from this condemnation.

But it is real. I know it from my own life — the things I am guilty of, the ways I have fallen short of what the people closest to me deserved, the moments I cannot undo. I am not free of those memories. I am free of their condemnation. And that distinction, which sounds almost too fine to matter, turns out to be the difference between a life spent in a crouch and a life spent standing upright. In fact, it is the freedom from condemnation and the unshackling from guilt that allowed me to write this book.

You do not have to be the sum of your worst moments. Your past is your story — it shaped you, it traveled with you, and it is part of who you are. But it is not your verdict. In Christ, the verdict has already been rendered: not guilty. Which means you are free — not to pretend the past didn't happen, but to stop letting it have the final word.

Divine Relief

The world is very good at punishing you. It has systems for it — legal ones, social ones, interpersonal ones. Break the law, and the state holds it over you, sometimes for the rest of your life. Break the unwritten rules — be the one who had the affair, who lost the business, who made the decision that hurt the people you loved — and society holds that over you too. The label sticks. The whisper follows you into new rooms. And the world, for all its talk of second chances, has a remarkably long memory.

What the world cannot do is restore you. It can punish, it can shame, it can demand restitution — but it has no mechanism for actually lifting the weight. It can sentence you, but it cannot set you free. That is simply beyond its power.

For what the world was powerless to do, God did.

He didn't send a program or a philosophy or a set of principles to live by. He sent a person. His son, in the flesh — fully human, fully present, acquainted with hunger and exhaustion and grief and betrayal. Not arriving as a distant authority figure handing down verdicts from on high, but as someone who sat at tables with the guilty, the broken, the publicly shamed, and the privately destroyed. Jesus gets a bad rap in some circles as a figure of judgment and restriction. But look at who he actually spent his time with. Tax collectors who had cheated their neighbors. Women whose reputations were in ruins. Men who had failed spectacularly and publicly. He was not repelled by any of it. He moved toward it.

And here is what he came to do — though it is bigger than the single line most people know. Yes, he came to forgive sins. But that is only the beginning. He came to establish a living connection between you and God — not a transaction you complete once and file away, but an ongoing relationship, a daily companionship, a presence that walks with you into the places you are most ashamed of and does not flinch.

He took upon himself what you deserved, so that you could be free. Not free in the abstract, but free in the specific — free from the guilt that has been rewriting your behavior for years, free from the condemnation that has been sitting on your chest, free from the performance of being someone who has it together when you know exactly what is hiding underneath.

Are Christians guilty? Yes. Absolutely, honestly, unambiguously yes. Are Christians condemned? No. And that gap — between guilt acknowledged and condemnation removed — is where the relief actually lives.

So how does it work in practice? Because saying "the guilt is gone" and actually experiencing that are two very different things. Here is the process, and it is worth taking seriously:

1. Bring your guilt to God. Not the edited version — the real one. He already knows it anyway.
2. You will both agree that you are guilty but not condemned. God does not pretend the thing didn't happen. He looks at it clearly and cancels it anyway.
3. God says, "When I see you, I do not see that thing you did that makes you guilty." That is not denial. That is what the cross accomplished.
4. God condemns the sin, not you. There is a difference, and it is everything.
5. God says, "Because I do not see your sin, I do not want you to see it either." This is the invitation to stop rehearsing what has already been forgiven.

6. And then — here is the part that is hardest to hear — God says, "But I do not want you condemning other people either. The person whose politics infuriate you, whose choices you find incomprehensible, whose life looks nothing like yours — I see them as my loving child. I don't condemn them. And I am asking you not to either."

7. Finally, if there is something you did that hurt another person, and it is within your power to make it right, God asks you to consider doing that.

This last step matters more than it might seem. The freedom the cross offers is not a license to leave wreckage behind you and walk away clean. Where repair is possible — a conversation that needs to happen, an acknowledgment that is owed, a relationship worth fighting to restore — the cross frees you to pursue it without shame. You are no longer defending yourself. You have nothing left to protect. That is actually a remarkably powerful place to act from.

God chooses to love you as if the sin never happened. Not because it didn't, but because he decided the relationship was worth more than the record. And if you follow these steps — not once, but repeatedly, as the guilt resurfaces and needs to be brought back to him again — something begins to shift. Slowly, sometimes imperceptibly, the weight lifts. Not all at once. But it lifts.

You were not made to carry this. You were made to be free. And the freedom is real, and it is available, and it has your name on it.

CHAPTER 6
"I DO"

In the movie " Moneyball, "Billy Beane asks Peter Brand one important question. "Do you believe in this thing or not?" Peter Brand answers, "I do."

At some point, every argument has to stop.

You can weigh the evidence indefinitely. You can read another book, attend another debate, follow another thread of objection down into its footnotes. But eventually — if the question is real and you are being honest with yourself — you have to decide where you land. Not with certainty. With enough. With sufficient reason to take a step.

This chapter is the case. Not the whole case — libraries have been written on this, and we have limited pages. But the essential structure of the argument, organized around the same mechanism you use to evaluate any claim: your belief hierarchy. The question at the end of it is the same one Billy Beane asked Peter Brand in a failing baseball operation in Oakland. Do you believe in this thing or not?

That is the only question that matters here. Everything else is just building toward it.

Your Belief Hierarchy

You do this every day without realizing it. Someone tells you something, and before you've even consciously processed it, your mind is already running it through a filter — weighing the source, cross-referencing what you already know, deciding how much stock to put in it. This filter is your belief hierarchy, and it operates almost automatically, shaped by everything that has happened to you up to this point.

The belief hierarchy is the internal system you use to decide whether something is true. It shifts depending on what's being claimed, who's doing the claiming, and how much the claim asks of you. Here are its five basic tenets — not ranked yet, just listed:

1. You read about it.
2. Someone who didn't witness it told you about it.
3. It was predicted, and now it has come to pass.
4. Someone who saw it told you about it.
5. You saw it face-to-face.

Let's put it to work with an example. Suppose you hear a report that a dog was spotted driving a car down your street. Your immediate reaction is disbelief — as it should be. But watch how your belief hierarchy kicks in. If your neighbor, who was standing on the sidewalk when it happened, calls you and says, "I watched a dog drive a car past my house" — that carries more weight than if you read a single sentence about it in a local blog. And if you had walked outside and seen it yourself, the question of belief wouldn't even arise. You saw it. Case closed.

Now flip it. Rank those same five tenets not by what's easiest to believe, but by what requires the most faith:

1. It was predicted, and now it has come to pass. (requires the most faith)

2. You read about it.
3. Someone who didn't witness it told you about it.
4. Someone who saw it told you about it.
5. You saw it face-to-face. (requires the least faith)

Seeing something yourself requires almost no faith — your own eyes are your most trusted source. But if someone told you six months ago that their dog was going to drive a car, and now they're telling you it happened? That requires a great deal of faith, and how much faith you have depends almost entirely on how much you trust that person. Low trust means the claim sits near the top of your faith-required scale — you'd need a lot of convincing. High trust brings it down considerably.

Your trust level is the variable that drives everything.

Now bring this to Jesus. When you consider the claim that God sent Jesus and is in human form — that he was born, lived, died, and rose again exactly as he said he would — your belief hierarchy engages whether you invite it to or not. You are not a firsthand witness to the resurrection. Neither am I. A woman named Mary Magdalene was. The disciples were. According to the historical record, hundreds of others claimed to be. So the question isn't just what you believe — it's how you're deciding what to believe, and whether the framework you're using is being applied consistently.

You've probably already run Jesus through your belief hierarchy and landed somewhere. Maybe you believe fully. Maybe you're skeptical. Maybe you've dismissed it without looking too closely at the evidence. What I'm asking is that you look at how you're deciding — and whether the standard you're applying to the resurrection is the same one you'd apply to anything else you consider credible.

Because the case for Jesus is stronger than most people realize, and your belief hierarchy, applied honestly, may take you somewhere unexpected.

It Was Predicted, and Now It has happened.

Consider what it would take to convince you. Not of something small — but of the biggest claim in human history. That God came to earth in human form, lived among ordinary people, was executed, and came back to life. That this was not a surprise ending but a plan announced in writing seven hundred years before it happened.

That is what the Hebrew prophets did. And if you're going to run Jesus through your belief hierarchy, honestly, this is where it gets interesting — because the category that requires the most faith is also the one with the most evidence behind it.

The prophets Isaiah, Malachi, and Haggai wrote about a coming figure centuries before Jesus was born. Not in vague, could-mean-anything language, but in specific, verifiable detail. Here is a condensed version of what they wrote — a Reader's Digest of three prophetic books, paraphrased to capture their meaning clearly:

> *Take comfort, says your God. The welfare payment plan you are on will be no more. The tight collar around your neck, the rod that you beat yourself with shame — I will break in two. I have pardoned you completely.*

> *I am going to shake things up. I will shake all nations, the earth, the dry places, and the wet places. Everything will be turned upside down. Everyone's thoughts about me will change. It will be dramatic for the whole earth — like a valley transformed into a mountain, or a hill flattened into a plain. The crooked places will be made straight.*

> *For I will suddenly appear on earth, and everyone, for eternity, will see it and know about it. You will finally see me for who I am. Everyone — all races, Jews and Gentiles, every nation — will see it. A voice in the wilderness will cry out: "Prepare the way of the Lord."*

A great light will shine. Those who are lost, the sinners and the downtrodden, the oppressed and the powerful — everyone who walks in darkness will see a great light. Those on their deathbed, those who think there is no hope left — they will see it too.

I will come in the form of a child, an infant born to a virgin. To those who follow him, they will call him Wonderful Counselor, Mighty King, Everlasting Father, Prince of Peace.

Now the prophets describe his life in detail — written, remember, seven hundred years before he was born:

He had difficulties as a young boy, like a tender shoot pushing up through dry ground. When he became a man, there was nothing unusual about his appearance — nothing that would make him stand out in a crowd. He was despised and rejected. Familiar with loneliness, with sorrow, with being passed over. His real friends were few.

Yet while he was on earth, strange things happened. Blind eyes were opened. Deaf ears were unplugged—people who had never walked suddenly leapt to their feet. The mute began to sing.

He was wrongly accused of a crime he did not commit, and he did not open his mouth to defend himself. Like a lamb led to slaughter, he said nothing. Not one friend stepped forward. Not one neighbor spoke up.

They killed him. They drove a spear into him to be certain. They beat him and crushed him, convinced they were carrying out justice — even God's justice. And as it happened, God laid all our failures upon him. His punishment would give us peace. His wounds would mend what was broken between God and us.

After they killed him, they buried him among criminals, though he had committed no crime. Yet he would see the light of life again. And in doing so, he would become the one who stands between us and judgment — interceding on our behalf.

So, has any of this come true?

Start with the sweeping claims. Has Jesus shaken things up? Has he turned history upside down? The answer is almost impossible to argue against. He is the most written about, most debated, most followed figure in human history. Drive through any town in the world, and you will see buildings with crosses. More people claim to follow Jesus today than follow any other religious figure. The movement that started with twelve ordinary people in an occupied corner of the Roman Empire now spans every continent, every culture, every language group on earth.

And it did not spread through military conquest or government mandate. It spread the way the prophets described — person-to-person, household-to-household, through the visible transformation of individual lives. The Roman Empire tried to stop it. Emperors threw Christians to lions. They burned them alive. They made sport of their deaths. And still it grew. Like a fire that cannot be extinguished, as one historian put it — except those words were written by the prophets seven centuries before Rome existed.

Now consider the personal details. Jesus grew up in the shadow. His mother claimed an angel had visited her — a story that, understandably, wore out its welcome quickly in a small town. He was widely believed to have been born out of wedlock, which in that culture was not a minor social inconvenience but a permanent mark. He was looked down upon, whispered about, dismissed. The first part of the prophecy — a tender shoot on dry ground, despised and rejected — fits his biography with uncomfortable precision.

His ministry followed the same script. He performed healings that his contemporaries, including hostile ones, did not deny. He was falsely accused. He was silent at his own trial. He was executed between criminals. And then — according to hundreds of eyewitnesses whose accounts were recorded within living memory of the events — he came back.

The prophecy said he would see the light of life again. It said he would become an intercessor, standing between humanity and judgment. It said his wounds would be the mechanism of our restoration.

Run that through your belief hierarchy. Seven hundred years of lead time. Specific details about his birth, his life, his death, his resurrection, and the global movement that would follow. Either the prophets got extraordinarily lucky across dozens of highly specific predictions — or something else is going on.

You get to decide. But decide honestly, with the same standard you'd apply to anything else you consider credible, because the evidence here is not as thin as you may have been told.

Someone Who Saw It told you about it.

The resurrection is the hinge on which everything turns. Not the Sermon on the Mount. Not the miracles. Not the teachings on forgiveness or the kingdom of God. Those things matter enormously — but if the resurrection didn't happen, they amount to the wisdom of a very good man who died and stayed dead. If it did happen, then everything Jesus said about himself is true, including his claim to be God stepping into human history. The resurrection is either the most important event that ever occurred, or the most successful fabrication. There is not much middle ground.

So let's treat it the way your belief hierarchy demands — as a historical claim that deserves honest scrutiny.

Start with Paul. Unlike Jesus, whose life was not documented by Roman record-keepers — Bethlehem was a small town, and peasant births weren't logged — Paul is extensively attested in the historical record. His letters to churches around the Mediterranean date to roughly 40 A.D., within a decade of the crucifixion. He is mentioned by Clement of Rome, by Ignatius of Antioch, and by Polycarp of Smyrna — three early Christian writers whose own historical existence is well established. This is not a figure conjured from thin air. Paul is one of the most documented individuals of the ancient world.

And Paul was not a believer. Not at first. His initial career was built on hunting down followers of Jesus and having them imprisoned and executed. He was a Roman Jew with official standing, and he used that standing to suppress what Rome considered a politically dangerous movement. He was, by his own description, the last person on earth who would have invented a resurrection story.

Then something happened on the road to Damascus. Paul describes it as an encounter with the risen Jesus — a blinding appearance that stopped him in his tracks and redirected the entire course of his life. Whatever you make of that claim, the behavioral evidence is striking. A man who had been systematically destroying the Christian movement abruptly became its most energetic advocate, eventually dying for it. People do not typically give their lives for something they know to be a lie.

After Damascus, Paul spent time with Peter, one of Jesus' closest disciples and a direct witness to the resurrection. From Peter, Paul learned the resurrection creed that was already circulating widely in Jerusalem. It is one of the earliest pieces of Christian writing we have, predating even Paul's letters. The creed is simple, almost rhythmic in its original language:

Christ died for our sins and was buried, He rose from the dead and was seen — He rose from the dead and was seen by many witnesses. (1 Corinthians 15:3:8 is a translated version from Greek of what Paul received)

This was not a document written for scholars. It was designed to be memorized and passed on by ordinary people, most of whom couldn't read. It spread because it was easy to carry, and because the people carrying it had either seen the risen Jesus themselves or knew personally someone who had.

Paul writes that more than five hundred people in Jerusalem claimed to have seen the resurrected Jesus. He makes this claim in a letter written while many of those witnesses were still alive — an extraordinarily bold move if the story were fabricated. In the ancient world, as today, the fastest way to discredit a claim is to produce a living witness who contradicts it. Paul was essentially saying: go ask them. They're still here.

None of them recanted. Not under social pressure, not under persecution, not under threat of death. The story held — not because people were gullible, but because the people telling it had seen something that could not be explained any other way, and they were willing to stake everything on it.

That is the testimony of the eyewitnesses. People who were there. People who touched the wounds, ate with him, and walked with him after the tomb was found empty. Your belief hierarchy asks how much weight to give someone who saw it firsthand and told you about it. Here, you don't have one witness. You have hundreds, and their testimony cost most of them everything.

What do you do with that?

Someone Who Did Not Witness It Told You About It

Here is what Paul was working with. No internet. No printing press. No mass media of any kind. No New Testament, no Gospels, no Bible — none of that existed yet. What he had was a creed, a handful of letters, and the testimony of people who had seen something so staggering that they couldn't stop talking about it. And with those limited tools, he carried the story of the resurrection across the entire Mediterranean world.

Think about what that actually required. Paul traveled to Corinth, Ephesus, Macedonia, Cyprus, and eventually Rome — on foot, by ship, across some of the most difficult terrain in the ancient world. He did this without institutional backing, without government support, and with active opposition from both Roman authorities and Jewish leadership. He was beaten, imprisoned, shipwrecked, and eventually executed. And he kept going, because the story he was carrying was not, in his mind, a story — it was a fact. Something had happened. He had encountered the risen Jesus himself. And he was not going to stop telling people about it.

The numbers that follow are worth sitting with. Around 33 A.D., shortly after the resurrection, there were roughly fifty Christians in Rome. Fifty people — a small dinner party by today's standards. By approximately 100 A.D., 70 years later, that number had grown to around 2,000. Three centuries after that, during the reign of Constantine, there were more than 33 million Christians in the Roman Empire alone, making it the dominant religion of the very empire that had executed its founder.

Fifty to thirty-three million. No mass communication. No social media campaign. No marketing budget. Just one person telling another, and that person telling the next, and so on — all the way around the Mediterranean and beyond.

So why did it spread? That is the question worth pressing on. Rome was no stranger to mythology. The pagan world was full of gods, full of stories about divine figures who died and returned. These were not naive people encountering the concept of resurrection for the first time. They had heard versions of it before, wrapped in various mythologies, and most of them had grown up dismissing those stories as exactly what they were — stories. So why did this one land differently?

The answer seems to be transformation. Not just the message, but the people carrying it. Early Christians behaved in ways that were genuinely strange by Roman standards. They showed no fear of death — not as bravado, but as settled conviction. When plague swept through Roman cities, most people fled. Christians stayed and cared for the sick, including people who weren't Christians. When they were dragged through the streets in Thessalonica, as Luke records in Acts, they didn't riot or retaliate. When Nero set Christians on fire in Rome to illuminate his garden parties, others watched — and some of those watching eventually asked what these people believed that made them capable of dying like that.

That is not the behavior of people who know they are perpetuating a fabrication. People do not go to the arena for a story they made up. They do not stay in plague-ridden cities for a legend. Something had happened — something that had reoriented their entire relationship to life and death — and the most stubborn evidence for it is not a document or an argument, but the way these people lived and the way they died.

Paul himself put it plainly. "For me to live is Christ, and to die is gain." That is not the statement of someone hedging their bets. It is the statement of someone who has looked at death and found it defanged — because the man who defeated it told him personally that the story doesn't end there.

That transformation — visible, unexplainable by ordinary means, compelling enough to turn the ancient world upside down — is still available. The rest of this book is about exactly that.

You Read About It in The Paper

Every generation has its defining document — the thing that gets passed around, argued over, built upon, and blamed for everything. For Western civilization, that document is the Bible. Love it or hate it, you cannot understand the last two thousand years of human history without it. It has shaped laws, toppled governments, inspired art, fueled wars, and quietly redirected more individual lives than any other text ever written. Whatever you think of its origins, its influence is simply not in dispute.

But the Bible as we know it did not drop from the sky fully formed. Before 325 A.D., there was no single agreed-upon collection of Christian writings. There were letters, gospels, accounts — circulating separately, in different communities, with varying degrees of authority. It was the Emperor Constantine who convened the First Council of Nicaea and brought church leaders from across the Mediterranean together to determine, among other things, which writings would be included and which would not. The choices they made were consequential. The resulting collection became the most printed, most translated, most widely distributed book in human history — with approximately 2.38 billion people today identifying as its followers.

That is worth pausing on. Not 2.38 billion people who have read it cover to cover, or who agree on every interpretation — but 2.38 billion people whose faith traces its roots back to a collection of documents assembled in the fourth century, describing events from the first. Whatever else you want to say about the Bible, the reach of the thing is extraordinary.

Now here is where I want to be careful — and direct. The Bible is not a religion. Religion is what people have done with the Bible, and frankly, some of it has been catastrophic. Wars launched in God's name. People condemned, excluded, and, worse, justified by scripture. Entire systems of oppression are propped up by selective quotation. I don't do religion. I am not interested in defending institutions that have used this book as a weapon. The Bible itself, read honestly and in full, does not support most of what has been done in its name.

There are also things the Bible does not address that we now know to be plainly wrong. It does not condemn slavery — a fact that has been used to cause enormous harm and cannot be glossed over. If you have walked away from the Bible partly because of how it has been wielded by people with an agenda — political, financial, or otherwise — I understand that, and I think your instinct was right. The problem was never the book. The problem was what certain people did with it.

What the Bible actually is, at its core, is a record of encounter. It is the account of people — flawed, complicated, often bewildered people — meeting God and trying to make sense of what happened. The Old Testament traces that encounter through the history of a people who kept turning away and being drawn back. The New Testament narrows the lens to a single figure — Jesus — and records what he said, what he did, how he died, and what happened three days later, as told by the people who were there.

The Gospels — Matthew, Mark, Luke, and John — are four separate accounts of Jesus' life, written by different authors for different audiences from different vantage points. They are not identical, which is actually evidence of their authenticity. Identical accounts suggest coordination. The variations in the Gospels suggest independent witnesses describing the same events from their own perspectives — which is exactly what eyewitness testimony looks like. The broad strokes are consistent. The peripheral details sometimes differ. That is how memory works.

Beyond the Gospels, the New Testament includes the letters of Paul — written earlier than the Gospels, within living memory of the events they describe — and the accounts of the early church in Acts. Together, they form a portrait of a movement that started with a handful of people in Jerusalem and, within a generation, had reached the far corners of the Roman Empire.

I came to this book not through tradition or obligation but through my own encounter with what it describes. I did not grow up being told I had to believe it. I read it, and something in it recognized me — or perhaps I recognized something in it. The Jesus described in these pages is not the figure that religion has often portrayed him as. He is humble, relentlessly inclusive, and consistently drawn to the people that respectable society has written off. He is harder on the religious establishment than on anyone else. He reserves his sharpest words not for sinners but for hypocrites — people who used the language of God to serve their own interests. Reading the Gospels with fresh eyes, without the overlay of everything that has been done in his name since, is a different experience than most people expect.

If you are finding something in this book that is resonating with you — something that feels less like new information and more like recognition — I would suggest that what you're experiencing is the living word doing what it has always done. It is not my writing that is doing that work. I am just pointing at something that was already there. The Bible is where you go to find it for yourself, in full, without my filter or anyone else's.

But before we get there — before we talk about what the Bible says and what it means for your life — there is more to establish about what was said and done on Jesus' behalf that the Bible itself does not record. The historical case for Jesus extends well beyond the pages of scripture. And that is where we are going next.

Seeing Jesus Face-To-Face

It is possible to see the risen Jesus face-to-face — not physically, not yet, but in the way that matters most right now. When I get to heaven, I will see him face-to-face in the fullest sense. That is available to you, too. But before that can happen, most of us have some work to do. We need to get rid of the Jesus we've been carrying around — the one that was handed to us by culture, by bad theology, by well-meaning people who got it wrong — and meet the actual one.

Leaving Your Jesus Behind

Let's start with a quick test. Which of the following did Jesus actually say in the Bible?

- Go to church on Sunday.
- Confess your sins every day.
- Try as hard as you can to be good.
- Give all your money to the poor.
- Pray for the dead.
- Don't do it — I'm watching you.
- You disappointed me.
- Be good, or else.
- If you are a sinner, no communion.
- Say three Hail Marys as penance.
- Follow Me.

If you picked the last one, you're right. He never said any of the others. Not one.

That gap — between what Jesus actually said and what has been attributed to him over two thousand years of religious tradition — is where many people get lost. They walk away from a version of Jesus that Jesus himself would not recognize. And honestly, walking away from that version makes sense. The problem is that they leave the real one behind.

Here is something worth understanding about Jesus that tends to get buried under layers of religious protocol: he was not interested in creating obstacles between people and God. He was interested in removing them. When he was on earth, he ignored religious convention so consistently and so publicly that it enraged the chief priests. He was a Jew who didn't follow their rules. His followers called him Rabbi — teacher, which was an additional insult to the establishment, since he wasn't teaching what they had authorized. And then he did something that, in their framework, was simply unforgivable: he forgave sins. Openly. Without ritual, without penance, without the proper channels. In Jewish law at the time, that was blasphemy — a crime punishable by death.

And who did he forgive? Who did he eat with, travel with, spend his time with? Not the respectable people. Not the religiously compliant. Tax collectors — who were despised as collaborators with Rome. Prostitutes. The ceremonially unclean. People that polite society had written off entirely. He was not merely tolerant of them — he was comfortable with them, in a way that left the religious establishment genuinely bewildered. As C.S. Lewis put it, he did not come to make bad people good. He came to make dead people live.

If Jesus showed up today, I don't think he'd spend much time in the affluent suburbs. He'd be in the neighborhoods most people avoid. He'd be with people navigating addiction, with gang members, with mothers who lost children to violence, with people whose lives don't fit neatly into any respectable category. He'd be with the gay community, with the transgender community, with the people that certain churches have spent considerable energy condemning. He would be completely at ease with all of them. And his message would be the same as it always was: love one another as I have loved you. Follow me into a different way of seeing, a different way of living.

If the Jesus you grew up with looks nothing like that — if he was primarily a figure of judgment, restriction, and political agenda —

then that Jesus needs to go. He was a construction. And it is worth asking who built him, and why.

Preconceived Notions About Jesus

Church culture has produced a remarkable number of versions of Jesus, most of them bearing only a passing resemblance to the one in the Gospels. This is not just a Catholic problem or a mainline Protestant problem. Megachurches have done plenty of damage here, too. Here are the most common distortions — the ones worth taking a wrecking ball to.

The Jesus who watches everything you do, then judges you. This version is always looking over your shoulder, cataloging your failures, waiting for you to slip up. It has to go. He is not here to catch you doing something wrong. He is here to help you find your way back after you do.

The Jesus who punishes you when you sin. You're in the middle of a health crisis, a financial collapse, a heartbreak — and someone tells you it's because of something you did. That is not Jesus. The world throws the storms. Jesus is the catcher's mitt for when they arrive.

The Distant Jesus. This version lives far away and can only be reached through enough prayers, enough candles, and enough ritual. Not true. He died and rose so that he could be with you — permanently, personally, without intermediary. He is not somewhere else. He is here.

The Bad Promise Keeper. You prayed for a healing that didn't come, a miracle that never arrived, and now you're angry because he didn't deliver. But look carefully at what he actually promised. He never promised an easy life, freedom from suffering, or protection from loss. The promise he made was for something on the other side of all of that — eternal life with him. That promise holds.

The Despondent Doctor. You prayed for someone you loved, and they died anyway. I am not going to minimize that. It is one of the hardest places a person can find themselves. What I will say is this: if you could see from his vantage point — where death is not the end of the story but a passage to something better — it might not change the grief, but it would change what the grief means.

The Ritual Guy. This version requires the right prayers, the right sacraments, and the right church attendance before he'll take you seriously. Wrong. He was allergic to religious protocol. The only thing he is actually interested in is you — not your performance, not your compliance, just you. The entry point is simply recognizing that you've turned away from God and believing in Jesus. That's it.

The Boogie Man. Someone dies, and you're told God needed another angel in heaven. Please discard this immediately. God does not cause death to fill a celestial quota. He is not the author of terminal illness or tragedy. His desire is for you to live — fully, richly, and ultimately forever.

The Guy with a Secret Plan for Your Life. There is no hidden blueprint, no specific career, city, or relationship that God has mapped out for you that you might accidentally miss. You choose your life. God offers guidance on how to live it well. The plan, if there is one, is the same for everyone — and Paul describes it in Galatians 5:22: love, joy, peace, patience, kindness, goodness, faithfulness, gentleness, self-control. Live from those things, and the path tends to take care of itself.

The Ultra-Conservative Right-Wing Jesus. Jesus was arguably the most apolitical figure in history. He was not a Republican or a Democrat. He was not a culture warrior. When the Pharisees tried to trap him on the question of taxes, he gave them an answer so precise and so elegant that it shut the conversation down entirely: give to

Caesar what is Caesar's, and to God what is God's. Neither side gets to claim him. Both sides keep trying anyway.

The Judge at the Gate. The fear that you will stand before him one day and be condemned for everything you've done — that is real, but it comes with a condition that is often left out: only if you don't believe in Jesus. Good works do not earn you entry. Belief does. And for those who believe, what awaits is not a reckoning but a homecoming — rewards based not on perfection but on faithfulness, on what you did with what you were given.

Can you let go of the Jesus that was assembled by people with agendas — political, financial, institutional — and consider the one who actually shows up in the Gospels? The one who moved toward the broken, forgave the unforgivable, infuriated the religious establishment, and died so that the distance between you and God could be permanently closed?

That is the Jesus worth meeting. And meeting him starts with clearing away everything in front of him.

Embrace the Moment.

Most people think of their life as a line — a beginning and an end, bookended by a birth certificate and a headstone. Everything that matters happens somewhere in between. When you embrace Jesus as who he claims to be — the Son of God, present on earth, risen from the dead — that line disappears. Your life is no longer a segment. It is placed in the context of eternity, and that changes everything about how you see the time you have right now.

Eternal life is not something that starts when you die. It starts the moment you believe. You are already in it. The people you have lost — your parents, your friends, the ones whose absence still catches you off guard on ordinary days — they are not gone. They are in what Jesus called the kingdom of God, and if they believed as you do, you will see them again. That is not a comforting sentiment invented to soften grief. It is the central promise of the resurrection — the one thing Jesus staked everything on, and the one thing worth holding onto when everything else feels uncertain.

And the kingdom is more inclusive than most churches would have you believe. The people already there — the ones who embraced Jesus and believed in him — are a remarkably diverse group. The murderers who turned to him in their final moments. The hypocrites who finally got honest. The gay and transgender people found in him the acceptance that the church often failed to offer. They are all there. Which means if you believe this to be true, the way you treat the people you have written off — the ones you've kept at arm's length for reasons of politics or morality or simple discomfort — has to change. You cannot hold onto eternity with one hand and contempt with the other.

When you begin to live inside that larger frame, the texture of ordinary life shifts. Your possessions start to look different — not worthless, but temporary, meaningful only when they are given away or used in the service of something that lasts. Your relationships deepen because you begin to understand that the people around you are not temporary either. The friendships built on genuine faith, the bonds forged through shared struggle and shared belief — those are not ending. They are just beginning. And when you see your relationships that way, forgiveness becomes easier. The trespasses that once felt enormous shrink when you hold them up against eternity. They are still real. But they are small.

If you are reading this in the middle of a terminal diagnosis — yours or someone you love — I want to speak directly to that. This is not the end. It is a transition, and I know that word can feel inadequate against the weight of what you are facing. But if you could see yourself the way Jesus sees you, you would see someone he is waiting to welcome home. And if you are the one standing beside the bed, watching someone you love move toward that transition, hold onto this: you will see them again. That promise is the one Jesus made and the one the resurrection secured.

God has known you longer than you have known yourself. He knitted you together before you were born, thought of you before you took your first breath, and has not stopped thinking of you since. You are not an accident of biology or circumstance. You are known, specifically and completely, by the one who made you — and that knowledge extends forward into eternity without interruption.

That is what it means to embrace the moment. Not to ignore the hardness of life, but to hold it inside a frame large enough to contain it. The end is not the end. And once that becomes real to you, the way you move through every ordinary day begins to change.

A Strange Invitation

Imagine you receive an invitation to a party. Not just any party — a celebration thrown specifically for you. No occasion listed, no dress code, no gift registry. Just your name on the envelope and a host who wants you there. Strange enough. But then you find out that the host is someone you've wronged — repeatedly, across years, in ways you haven't fully accounted for. And yet the invitation still stands. No apology required at the door. No cover charge. No list of conditions you have to meet before you're allowed in. Just come.

That is the invitation Jesus extends. And it is, by any ordinary measure, a deeply strange one.

There is no quid pro quo here. No elaborate ritual required, no special prayer with the right words in the right order. It doesn't matter where you are reading this — at a coffee shop on a quiet morning, or in a prison cell, or in a hospital waiting room. The invitation is the same. If you can say, honestly, "I do believe" — if you can acknowledge that you have turned away from God and are willing to turn back — you are in. Not on probation. Not conditionally. In.

And here is something worth sitting with. That hollow feeling you carry — the low-grade emptiness that surfaces in quiet moments, the sadness that sometimes lives just behind your eyes, the sense that something is missing and you can't quite name it — that is not a personal failing. It is not evidence that something is wrong with you. It is evidence that you were built for something more than this world can offer. You were made for another place — one without the injustice and grief and disease and disappointment that this one is saturated with. The ache you feel is not a malfunction. It is a homing signal.

God is not indifferent to that ache. He is grieved by it. He watched you drift, watched the sadness accumulate, watched the weight of it reshape the way you move through your days. And rather than issuing a list of requirements for you to meet before he'd consider helping, he sent his son — in-the-flesh into the mess, so that you could see your situation from a completely different angle.

Here is what actually happened when you said yes to Jesus, or when you consider saying yes now. Your sins were forgiven — yes, that part is true, and it matters. But something larger happened. Your name was written into the book of life. That is not a metaphor for feeling better about yourself. It means that you are now held — not by this world, not by your worst decisions, not by your death — but by the one who was there before any of it and will be there long after. You cannot be taken captive by what this world throws at you, because you no longer belong entirely to it.

Paul understood this. After wrestling with it — and he did wrestle with it, this former persecutor of Christians who had more reasons than most to feel the weight of his own guilt — he arrived somewhere that most people never reach. He looked death in the face and asked, without irony: "Oh death, where is your sting?" That is not bravado. That is what happens to a person who has genuinely internalized the resurrection. Death loses its power to terrify when you understand that it is not the end of your story — it is a transition point within a story that has no ending.

Without Jesus, you are fully inside this world — subject to its logic, its cruelties, its timeline, its verdict on who you are and what you're worth. Your ability to cope with its darkness is limited to what the world itself can offer, which is not much. And then it ends, and you end with it. That is one way to live. Many people do.

But Jesus offers a different position entirely. Not escape from the world — you are still in it, still subject to its difficulties, still going to suffer and grieve and lose things you love. But you are no longer of it. You stand beside it rather than inside it. You can look at its suffering with genuine compassion rather than despair, because you know it is not the whole story. You can face your own death — or the death of someone you love — without being destroyed by it, because you know that death is a point in time, not a final verdict.

This invitation is for anyone. It is for the person who was handed Sunday school answers to adult questions and walked away frustrated. It is for the person who tried faith once and felt nothing. It is for the person who is angry at God, or has given up on God, or isn't sure God exists at all but feels something pulling at them anyway — some persistent, low-level tug that won't quite go away no matter how determinedly they ignore it.

That tug might be the invitation itself.

If you find yourself in that last category — if you feel like something is wrong, like you keep falling short of your own standards, like you can't seem to get traction no matter how hard you try — that might not be a sign that you are beyond help. It might be a sign that you are being looked for. Jesus has a way of finding people at exactly the point where their own resources have run out. That is not a coincidence. It is, if anything, his preferred method.

C.S. Lewis put it this way: "I believe in Christianity as I believe that the sun has risen — not only because I see it, but because by it I see everything else." That is what the faith lens does, slowly and over time. It doesn't just give you new beliefs. It gives you new eyes. And once you begin to see through them, the world looks different — not easier, but clearer. More bearable. More meaningful. And for the first time, genuinely full of hope.

The invitation is open. It has your name on it. And the host has been waiting a long time for you to walk through the door.

CHAPTER 7
LETTING THE DAYS GO BY

This chapter is about direction. Not the grand, dramatic kind — not a sudden crisis or a flash of obvious failure — but the quiet, everyday kind that happens when we stop paying attention to where we are headed. It is about what letting the days go by means and what it costs. It is also about what Jesus said to people who were lost and didn't know it yet — and what he offers to anyone willing to consider a different road. If you have ever arrived somewhere in life and wondered how you got there, this chapter is for you.

Accidental Traveler

There is something almost miraculous about GPS. I remember when getting lost meant pulling over, unfolding a crumpled map, and hoping for the best. Now, the moment I veer off course, a calm voice tells me how to find my way back. It's quick, it's simple, and within minutes, I'm headed in the right direction again.

Each of us is a traveler. Your life is moving somewhere — toward something. The question is not whether you will arrive somewhere, but whether you will arrive at a place you actually wanted to go.

The tricky part is that getting lost in life is far harder to detect than getting lost on a road. You don't hear a soft voice recalculating. Life just keeps moving. And sometimes you meet someone — or perhaps you recognize yourself — who has been drifting along for years, seemingly content, only to arrive at a dead end and look genuinely surprised. How did I get here? The days just... went by.

I have watched good people take small detours that quietly became the main road. What began as a casual weekend at the casino became a consuming habit. A harmless flirtation at work became something that destroyed a family. A little recreational spending became debt that shadowed everything. None of these people woke up one morning and decided to ruin their lives. They simply let the days go by, and the detour became their direction. Sometimes getting lost is more subtle. People become lost in their vocation, in their marriage, and in their friendships. Perhaps it's just a feeling you have that you are missing direction in life. But you just plot along… letting the days go by.

And the painful thing is, you rarely know the moment you got lost. There's no alert, no notification. It might be months before the fog lifts, or it might be years. In the meantime, you keep going — doing the same things, reinforcing the same patterns — perfectly content in the wrong direction. Until one day, something catches up with you.

When that moment arrives, it can feel crushing — lost, isolated, hollowed out. And here's the difficult truth: this is exactly where a world that does not love you wants you to land. The world is very good at selling a version of happiness built on advancement, achievement, and accumulation. It tells you that winning means getting ahead, having more, and being admired. But that kind of happiness is fragile. When trouble comes — and it always does — those things offer no shelter.

When you end up somewhere you never intended, there is grief — for you, and quietly, for the heavenly Father who loves you more than you know. The grief is not just over the destination; it's over all the things that passed by unnoticed. You miss your children growing up. Friendships you never nurtured. Seasons of life you can't recover. A marriage that deserved more of you.

Hindsight arrives with a kind of cruel clarity. "I should have seen this coming," you tell yourself. And your friends, who honestly saw it long before you did, nod quietly. But here is something worth noticing: those same friends who spotted the warning signs in your life are almost certainly blind to the very same patterns in their own. Jesus understood this perfectly. He asked, gently but pointedly, why we are so quick to notice the speck in someone else's eye while ignoring the plank in our own.

Or perhaps it's something you could see, but chose not to. Your friends tried to reach you. You sensed the truth yourself. But looking at it directly felt like too much, so you kept moving. And then you arrived somewhere you never planned to be — and the surprise on your face surprised even you.

So you take stock. You reach out — maybe to a counselor, maybe to a trusted friend. And that is a good and honest thing to do. But the deeper truth is this: the patterns that led you here are not easily untangled. They were woven into you long before you noticed them. You can work through them, grow through them, even help others because of them — but you cannot simply erase them. Our past shapes the lens through which we see everything, including what we trust.

But here is the good news, and it is genuinely good: that lens does not have to define you. It does not have the final word. When we are lost on the road, we do not ask someone to magically undo our wrong turns. We ask for a new direction. That is what Jesus offers. Not a miraculous erasure of the mess, but a new heading — a recalibration of where we are pointed and why. Perhaps a new lens.

Maybe that's part of why you walked away from Jesus. Because he did not fix things the way you hoped. The marriage did not mend.

The habit did not disappear. The prayer felt unanswered. And if Jesus is not a quick fix, what is the point? But consider this: a truly good friend, a wise counselor, a trusted mentor — none of them promise to reach in and undo your problems either. What they offer is something more lasting: a new way of seeing, a different way of walking, a reorientation of the heart. That is what Jesus came to offer. Not a magic lamp, but a light for the road ahead.

Accidental Builder

Here is a question worth sitting with: Do you build your life, or does life simply happen to you? Most of us would like to believe we are the architects of our own story. We set goals, make plans, choose a partner, and build a career. And yet, even the most deliberate among us — those who did everything right by the world's standards, earned the degrees, landed the jobs, built the family — can still find themselves at a dead end, sitting in the rubble of something they carefully constructed and wondering how it fell apart. When that happens, it is tempting to say, "This must be the life God planned for me." But more often than not, the road you are on was one you started down long before you noticed. And if we are honest, the question is not just whether you planned your life — it is what you built it on, and whether that foundation was sound.

Arthur C. Brooks, in his thoughtful book From Strength to Strength, takes on the world's standard formula for happiness — work hard, follow the rules, catch a few breaks, retire, and die content. His conclusion? It does not hold up. Drawing on the research of Harvard psychologist Raymond Cattell, Brooks points to two forms of intelligence that shape a fulfilling life. The first, fluid intelligence, is the sharp, generative energy of your younger years — the drive that builds careers and establishes families. It peaks somewhere in your late thirties or early forties, then begins to fade. The second, crystallized intelligence, is what grows in its place: the wisdom to teach, to synthesize, to recognize patterns and pass on what you have learned. Brooks argues that the people who find genuine happiness are those who learn to transition gracefully between these two — from building for themselves in their thirties and forties, to building for others in their fifties and beyond. There is real wisdom here. But I keep thinking about the people who never quite found their footing in the first place — the ones who are lost but do not yet know it. How do they begin to build something that will last? We will return to that question in the chapter What Will Your Verse Be?

The search for happiness is harder than it looks. Gallup CEO Jon Clifton, in his book Blind Spot, tracked a troubling rise in global unhappiness — from roughly one in four people in 2006 to one in three by 2021. His prescription is that governments should treat unhappiness the way they treat economic data: as a crisis worth solving. I understand the concern, but I respectfully part ways with the solution. No government program has ever filled the hollow place in a human soul, and I do not believe one ever will. The deeper irony is that the very root of the unhappiness Clifton describes — the sense that others have more, live better, deserve less — is something God addressed long ago. Do not covet. Do not measure your life against your neighbor's. Someone will always have more, and someone will always have less. If your contentment depends on that comparison, you will never arrive. So if not the government, then who? What source of authority is actually trustworthy enough to build a life on?

Jesus knew all of this about us long before we knew it about ourselves. He knew we would drift. He knew we would hunger for something we could not name. He knew the soul's particular ache — that feeling of being misdirected, hollow, full of quiet regrets. And he knew that a life lived without examining where it is headed would eventually run out of road. After his Sermon on the Mount, in Matthew 7:24, he offers this:

"Everyone, then, who hears these words of mine and acts on them will be like a wise man who built his house on a rock."

Jesus is drawing on something every craftsman in his audience would have understood. In the ancient world, building on rock was slow, difficult, and costly work. It required patience, deliberation, and a willingness to delay gratification. The man who chose rock was playing the long game. He was developing what Brooks might call fluid intelligence — gathering wisdom through experience, learning what works and what does not — and later crystallized intelligence — investing in others and passing on what he had learned. This is not just a lesson in construction. It is a picture of how a life is wisely built. Jesus continues:

"The rain fell, the floods came, and the winds blew and beat on that house, but it did not fall because it had been founded on rock."

In other words, when life's storms arrive — and they will — a life built on something solid will hold. The foundation is not a guarantee against hardship. It is a guarantee that the hardship will not destroy you. Jesus then turns the picture over:

"And everyone who hears these words of mine and does not act on them will be like a foolish man who built his house on sand."

Jesus is asking something of us here. Not passive belief, but active engagement with the direction of our lives. The foolish man's mistake was not that he lacked ambition or intelligence — it was that he built without thinking about what would happen when the weather changed. Sand is easy. Sand is fast. Sand requires no real sacrifice. But it will not hold when the rains come. And the foolish man, comfortable in the good weather, simply never imagined that the good weather would not last. Then Jesus finishes:

"The rain fell, and the floods came, and the winds blew and beat against that house, and it fell — and great was its fall!"

When the storm came for the foolish man, it did not just bring discomfort — it brought collapse. And in that collapse, others were caught in the wreckage too. Now he wants a quick fix. A shortcut back to solid ground. But there is none. The work of rebuilding is real and slow, just like the work of building well in the first place. What I find deeply comforting, though, is that God responds to our poor choices the way any loving father responds to a child who has fallen — not by engineering the fall, not by walking away, but by being there when you hit the ground. God does not throw the storms. He holds out a catcher's mitt in Jesus, ready to receive whatever broken thing you bring him.

Here is something important to notice: both the wise man and the foolish man faced the storm. Following Jesus does not exempt you from hardship. And maybe that is part of why you walked away. You did everything right. You prayed. You believed. You tried to be good. And the storm came anyway, while others who seemed not to pray glided through life unscathed. That is a real and painful thing to wrestle with. I understand why it might have led you to conclude that God is absent, or indifferent, or simply not there. But Jesus told us from the beginning: the storm will come. He never promised a life without rain. What he offered was a foundation that does not crumble when it does. And sadly, that message has been buried under layers of bad doctrine, prosperity theology, and well-meaning people who preached a gospel of rewards for obedience. That is not the gospel. Jesus is not asking for your compliance. He is asking for your heart. He wants a relationship with you — because he does not want you to be alone when the winds rise.

I Can't Get No

There is a difference between happiness and satisfaction that is worth slowing down to consider. Happiness is a mood — it rises and falls with circumstances, good news, a pleasant afternoon, a meal you loved. Satisfaction is something quieter and more durable. You can be going through a genuinely difficult stretch and still feel, underneath it all, that your life is headed somewhere good. Conversely, you can have every comfort the world offers and feel, in the stillness of a Tuesday evening, that something essential is missing.

And there is the rub.

Take something simple: pizza. I love pizza. Genuinely, unreservedly love it. But no matter how good it is, the pleasure fades. The same is true for the round of golf, the new car, the vacation you looked forward to for months. These things bring genuine joy in the moment — and that is not nothing. But they do not stay with you. The feeling drifts away, and you find yourself reaching for the next thing.

The world is very skilled at selling us euphoria — fine restaurants, expensive vacations, beautiful things. And those pleasures are real while they last. But what remains when the excitement fades? A depreciating asset. A few photographs. Sometimes debt. True satisfaction is different. It does not require a special occasion. It does not expire. It is a companion that stays.

Life satisfaction does not require things, or events, or moments of peak experience. It is the quiet, settled feeling of having built something real — of having lived with intention, of arriving somewhere close to where you hoped to be, with few regrets and open hands. It is the one thing the foolish man never finds, because he is always thinking only about today.

The wise person knows that satisfaction cannot be found in the things this world is selling. It comes from somewhere deeper — from choices that outlast the moment, from a way of living that transcends circumstances. If you find yourself on a path marked by regret and quiet emptiness, that may simply be an invitation to consider a different road altogether. One that is not built on what the world promises, but on something more enduring. This is part of why what Jesus said was so compelling, and why it still is.

Following Jesus does not mean withdrawing from the world or becoming someone unrecognizable. It means reorienting your compass. It means doing, in many cases, the quiet opposite of what the world tells you is the path to happiness. Jesus laid this out with remarkable clarity in the Sermon on the Mount, in Matthew 5:

"Blessed are the poor in spirit, for theirs is the kingdom of heaven."

Jesus says something surprising here: being low in spirit, feeling the weight of your own insufficiency, is actually the beginning of something good. Why? Because it is in those moments that we stop pretending we have it all together. We become, perhaps for the first time, genuinely open to receiving help from outside ourselves. The world will tell you to buy something, distract yourself, push through. Jesus says, " Come as you are, empty-handed, and let that emptiness draw you to the one who can fill it.

Notice how differently the world responds to that same low feeling. It hands you a distraction — something shiny, something exciting, something that will hold your attention just long enough to avoid the real question. And then the novelty fades, and you are back where you started. God's counsel is more direct and more honest: stop measuring your life against your neighbor's. Someone will always have more. Someone will always seem further along. Comparison is a road that leads nowhere good. When you feel that hollow sadness, what is your first instinct? A purchase? A scroll through someone else's highlight reel? Or a genuine, honest turn toward God? A person whose faith lens is beginning to shift will increasingly find themselves choosing the latter.

"Blessed are those who mourn, for they will be comforted."

Can you be blessed while mourning? Jesus says yes, though I do not think he means you will be skipping through it. What he seems to be pointing to is the kind of comfort that comes when we allow ourselves to be fully present in grief — not hiding from it, not rushing past it, but entering it with others who are not afraid of it either. The people who are most comforted in sorrow are generally those who have learned to be present for others in theirs. They have built the kind of relationships where grief is not met with awkward silence but with quiet, steady presence. What does your inner circle look like? Are those people able to sit with you in the hard things? Do they face life as we discussed in chapter two — holding the brutal reality in one hand and the hope of eternity in the other?

The hope of eternal life changes the way we face death — our own and others'. Without it, death becomes something to be managed, avoided in conversation, dressed up, and kept at arm's length. I know this from the inside. When I was diagnosed with prostate cancer, I found something unexpected: I was at peace with the possibility of going home to God. What I prayed for was not healing, but company. I did not want to go through it alone. And within what felt like days, God brought men into my life who were walking the same road — through my Bible study group, through quiet connections I could not have engineered. None of us was thrilled about where we might be headed. But we were not alone. That is a particular kind of comfort that no earthly thing can replicate — the knowledge that you are truly, deeply loved.

"Blessed are the meek, for they will inherit the earth."

Meekness sounds, to modern ears, like a polite word for weakness. But I think Jesus means something far richer. The fool charges through life, certain that he is the master of his circumstances. The wise person has come to understand her limitations. Not as a defeat, but as wisdom. She has sat with her failures long enough to learn from them. She knows the difference between what she caused and what simply happened to her. That discernment is not weakness. It is one of the most powerful things a person can carry.

When you begin to see through the lens of Jesus, you discover that humility is not a diminishment — it is a kind of strength that the world rarely recognizes until it is too late. Dr. Hannah Rose, writing for the National Health Service, put it this way in her piece on the paradox of humility: those who are humble typically have healthy self-esteem, but without the need to broadcast it. They tend to be more courteous, more attuned to others, and far less prone to the kind of arrogance that quietly drives people away.

"Blessed are those who thirst and hunger for righteousness, for they will be filled."

When Jesus speaks of righteousness here, he is not primarily talking about moral perfectionism. He is talking about being rightly related to God and to the people around you. A person who is righteous in this sense has done the internal work. They carry no old scores. They have forgiven, even those who have not asked to be forgiven, even those who may never ask. There is a settled freedom in that kind of living.

Being righteous in this sense means making the choice that will cost you today but serve you and others well tomorrow. It means releasing yourself from the weight of "if only" and "I should have." It means choosing not to carry bitterness, not because the wrong done to you was small, but because the weight of resentment is simply too heavy to bear for long. I have never met a truly happy person who also harbors deep grudges. The two do not coexist well.

"Blessed are the merciful, for they will be shown mercy."

Mercy is righteousness in motion. It is choosing, again and again, to be generous in your relationships — to overlook the slight, to forgive without waiting for the apology, to release the other person before they have earned it. The merciful do not tally wrongs. They do not fantasize about the moment justice finally arrives in their favor. I have never met someone who was genuinely at peace with their life who also carried long, slow grudges. It simply does not happen. Mercy sets the one who offers it free.

"Blessed are the pure in heart, for they will see God."

Purity of heart is the aspiration to live free from the things that quietly damage us and those we love. I will be honest — I strive for it and fall short regularly. What gives me peace is this: if you have trusted Jesus, the heavenly consequences of your sin have been covered. The cross took care of that. But the earthly consequences? Those are still real. The cross does not undo the damage done by the choices you made on that business trip, or by what you allowed to take root in your heart late at night, or by the words spoken in anger that you cannot retrieve. Jesus saves you from condemnation. He does not always save you from the consequences. And those consequences — to relationships, to your own soul, to the people who love you — are worth taking seriously.

Those choices quietly redirect your path. You will still arrive somewhere — you always do. But where you land will not be the place you hoped for. Jesus calls us to purity of heart not as an arbitrary requirement, but out of love — for your sake, and for the sake of everyone who is building a life alongside yours.

"Blessed are the peacemakers, for they will be called children of God."

I have never in my life encountered an angry, bitter peacemaker. The two simply do not go together. The people I know who have the gift of reconciliation — who can walk into a fractured relationship and begin to gently repair it — are, almost without exception, people who have lived deeply and learned from their own wounds. They have high crystallized intelligence. They know what it costs to be estranged, so they are not cavalier about conflict. And they are, by and large, the most contented people I know.

I found myself once in the middle of a quiet conflict — two people speaking poorly of each other to me, each certain the other was to blame. I chose not to carry either story. Instead, I told each one something true and good about the other. I did not take sides. I did not rehearse grievances. And in time, without any formal intervention, the two found their way back to each other. I offer this not as a point of pride — I do not always get it right, and I am not always the peacemaker I aspire to be — but as evidence that small acts of mercy and fairness have a longer reach than we often realize.

"Blessed are those that are persecuted because of righteousness, for theirs is the kingdom of heaven."

I will be honest: I enjoy being right. There is real pleasure in that moment when the answer becomes clear, and you were the one who saw it. But standing up for what you believe when it costs you something — when your convictions make you an outlier, when your faith marks you as different — that is a different kind of challenge entirely.

No one welcomes rejection. And yet the courage of conviction — standing for something true even when it draws criticism, living differently because you genuinely believe it is better — is one of the most dignifying things a person can do. If you follow Jesus, you will at some point experience what it means to be misunderstood, perhaps even by people you love. That discomfort is real. But condemnation passes. The peace that comes from being rightly oriented — from knowing whose you are and where you are headed — that is a companion for the whole of life.

That is a great deal to hold. Let the spirit feel low. Be emotionally present. Choose humility. Pursue righteousness and mercy. Live with purity. Make peace. Stand firm when it costs you. These are the materials for building a life on a rock. I know what some of you are thinking: this is too much. And you are right that I do not know your situation — the disease, the marriage that is barely holding, the financial weight, the children who are not where you hoped they would be. I do not know what you are carrying. I would never pretend to. But I will say this: you cannot achieve deep, lasting satisfaction on your own. The world will not help you find it. It is not interested in your contentment. It is interested in your consumption.

The apostle Paul faced circumstances that would have broken most of us. He knew hunger and abundance, imprisonment and freedom, persecution and peace. And from that experience, he wrote something remarkable to the church in Philippi. He told them he had learned a secret — a way of being content in any and every situation, regardless of what the circumstances happened to be. Not a technique. Not a philosophy. A secret. So what was it?

The Secret

There is a historical phenomenon worth pausing over. Within a few decades of the crucifixion of an obscure carpenter in a backwater province of the Roman Empire, a movement built around his name had spread from Jerusalem to Antioch, Cyprus, Ephesus, Philippi, Macedonia, Thessalonica, Syracuse, and Rome. Christianity grew at roughly 40 percent per decade — reaching perhaps 34 million people by A.D. 40, and at least 10 percent of the Roman Empire by A.D. 350. All of this without mass communication, without institutional infrastructure, without political backing. The movement spread quietly, person to person, through households and friendships. What could possibly explain it? A crucified man who was said to have risen from the dead. That is what started all of this.

Historians have long debated what drove that growth, but many point to the same thing: transformation. Not doctrine, not social programs, not charismatic leadership alone — but the visible, undeniable transformation of individual lives. That transformation was compelling enough that people were willing to die for it. And not just in the first century; Christians are still being persecuted and dying for their faith today, in places that rarely make the headlines. They refused to deny Jesus. They refused to surrender the secret. What changed them so completely? And if we could find it — if we could actually lay hold of what Paul called the secret of contentment — would it change us too? Would it bring us closer to the meaning and purpose we have been searching for all along?

Let's trace how this transformation actually happens. To do that, we need to return to something we explored in the first chapter: the distinction between body, soul, and spirit. C.S. Lewis put it simply: you are a soul who happens to have a body. Your body is not you. It is the vessel — aging, changing, subject to all the indignities and limitations of physical existence. Whether it is strong or frail, young or old, conventionally attractive or not, that is the body. The soul is the conscious, thinking, feeling you. And then there is the spirit, which is harder to locate. John the Apostle wrote that what is born of flesh is flesh, and what is born of spirit is spirit — they are distinct categories. The spirit communicates with the soul, but it operates below the surface, in what we might call the unconscious. You cannot force it into view. But its influence is real.

When you said "I do" to Jesus — when you genuinely opened yourself to him — something happened that is difficult to explain but very real. The power of God, the Spirit of Jesus, took up residence in you. Perhaps your soul felt it in that moment. Perhaps it was quieter than you expected. But the transaction was made.

Notice what did not change. If you were bad at math before, you are still bad at math. If you had wrinkles, they're still there. Who you are attracted to, what you are good at, what your body looks like — none of that is the point of what happened. The change was not in the body, and it was not even a change in the soul. It was something new in the spirit.

Paul writes in 2 Corinthians 5:17 that if anyone is in Christ, there is a new creation — the old has gone, the new has come. Not a new body, not a reset of your personality, but a new spirit. The Spirit of God now lives in you, reaching toward the Father with a kind of longing that is hard to articulate but unmistakable when it stirs. You belong to God now. He claims you as his own. You are written into the book of life — and nothing, not the darkness of this world, not your worst days, not your greatest failures, can separate you from him. What you could never achieve through effort or good behavior, God accomplished for you. That is not a small thing.

Maybe that is part of why you left, or why you hesitated. You were hoping for something faster — a sign, a miracle, a perceptible shift. But God did not promise speed. He promised movement. A gradual, sometimes imperceptible repositioning of the lens through which you see everything — your circumstances, your pain, the world's brokenness — until you begin to see it all, slowly, through his eyes.

As trust grows, something accumulates in you. God deposits something in your heart that gradually, over years and seasons, shifts the way you see. Not a dramatic overhaul, but a slow reorientation — the way your eyes adjust as you walk from a bright room into a dimly lit one, until you can see things you could not see before. This is, in many ways, what your life is actually for. Not to accumulate, not to achieve, but to build trust in Jesus and let that trust reshape your vision. This is why you read, study, pray, and sit in community with others who are on the same road.

But here is where many of us get stuck. I still stumble. I know

Christians who talk beautifully about grace and treat people terribly. I have been the hypocrite myself more times than I care to count. Does that mean the transformation has failed? Not at all.

The cross is the answer to that question. It is the tool you reach for when you have gone off course — not to beat yourself with it, but to release the guilt and shame that would otherwise trap you there. You stumbled. You acknowledge it. You turn around and get back on the road. That is not failure. That is the Christian life, honestly lived.

Stumbling is not a disqualification. Your spirit and God's Spirit share the same space in your soul, and because you are free — genuinely, irrevocably free — you will sometimes turn away from the Spirit's quiet guidance and follow your own instincts instead. Your own instincts are often wrong, and they tend to get you into the kind of trouble that takes years to untangle. But the Spirit is patient. It is always there, always ready to redirect, always teaching with the wisdom of Jesus — if you are willing to listen.

Oscar Wilde once observed that the only difference between a saint and a sinner is that every saint has a past and every sinner has a future. There is grace in that. But grace is not an invitation to drift. There are many people who have said "I do believe" and meant it — and then let the days go by without acting on it. They will not lose eternity over that. But they may lose the life they could have had here. They may wake up one day somewhere they never intended to be, wondering how the days disappeared.

Spiritual Superhighway

So how do you know whether you are on the right track? Here is a curious thing about mirrors: when you look into one, you see a reflection — but it is reversed, incomplete. You cannot fully see yourself from the inside. You need someone else for that. A friend who knows you well, a mentor who has walked this road longer, a community that holds up an honest image of who you are becoming. You learn to trust the mirror not because it flatters you, but because it tells the truth.

The Bible offers what no mirror can: a picture of who you are in the spirit, and who you are becoming. It is the place where spiritual truth is discerned, where the mind begins to be genuinely renewed, where transformation takes root and grows. The Apostle Paul, in Galatians 5, describes what that transformation looks like in practice. He calls them the fruits of the Spirit: love, joy, peace, patience — even for the people who make patience feel impossible — kindness, generosity, faithfulness, gentleness, and self-control. These are not a checklist. They are the natural output of a life that is growing in the right direction. And please — do not turn them into a competition. The moment you start keeping score of your spiritual fruit compared to someone else's, you have missed the point entirely.

On the other side of that picture, Paul describes the fruits of the flesh — the patterns of living that quietly destroy what we are trying to build. Sexual immorality, in all its forms, tends to unravel relationships and carry consequences we did not anticipate. Overindulgence — in alcohol, in substances, in anything that numbs or controls us — pulls us off course. Placing anything at the center of your life that was not made to bear that weight — a celebrity, a career, a romance, an ideology — will disappoint you and erode your closest relationships. Hostility toward people whose politics or identity differ from yours does not make you look principled; it makes you look small, and it wounds real people in the process.

Gossip and division quietly and effectively poison the community. And jealousy — transparent to everyone who is watching, even when we think we have hidden it — makes us miserable and unattractive to be around. These are not arbitrary rules. They are descriptions of behaviors that lead, consistently and predictably, away from the life you actually want.

I know. This is a lot. It is hard. You will stumble, and sometimes you will stumble spectacularly. Would God really be impressed by your white-knuckled effort to be good — only to watch you fall again? Here is the honest answer: God is not keeping score the way you fear. He is not cataloging your failures with growing disappointment. When you look at yourself through the eyes of a God who is beyond all comprehension, what you find is not a ledger. You find a father. And that is precisely why we have the cross. The cross absorbs the guilt and the shame — not just some of it, all of it. It puts you back on the right road without condemnation. God has forgotten it. He will not bring it up again. And perhaps, with some practice, you can learn to do the same.

When you die, God will not recite your failures back to you. He cannot hold them against you — they have been dealt with. The cross saw to that. The record is clean. You do not need to keep rehearsing what has already been forgiven.

But does this mean that grace gives us license to live however we please? To indulge every impulse and simply apply the cross at the end? Paul wrestled with exactly this question in Romans 6. "Should we continue in sin so that grace may increase?" And his answer was unequivocal: by no means.

Here is why. As the Spirit grows in you and your faith lens gradually shifts toward God's perspective, your appetite for things that harm you naturally diminishes. Not overnight, and not without struggle — but the direction of desire slowly changes. There is also the practical reality: sin takes you somewhere. And as we have spent this entire chapter exploring, where you end up matters enormously. Think of it this way. Imagine two pools in your backyard. One is clear, cool, and inviting. The other is murky and thick with algae — something is moving in there, and you are not sure it is friendly. And yet, because the murky pool is familiar, because you have spent years wading in it, some part of you is still drawn to it.

But as you spend more time in the clear pool, you find that it becomes comfortable. The thing in the murky water that used to pull you in — it no longer has the same hold. You still visit the muck pool sometimes. I do. You will too. But over time, with Jesus as a closer and closer companion, the desire fades — not because of rules or fear, but because you do not want to do something that grieves him. He will not, however, shield you from the consequences of the times you choose the muck. Those consequences — to your health, your relationships, your work, your family — are real, and they are yours to carry. That is simply part of being free.

Here is something that surprises many Christians when they hear it for the first time. When you said "I do believe," Jesus fulfilled the law on your behalf — including the Ten Commandments. You are no longer under that law as an external obligation. What he did instead was write it into your heart. You know, in the quiet of your conscience, when you have broken one of them. Every Christian has felt that interior nudge of the Spirit. Jesus distilled the whole of the commandments into three simple guides:

- Do nothing that would hurt God.
- Do nothing that would hurt another person.
- Do nothing that hurts yourself.

The Old Testament is full of laws that no human being could fully keep — which is precisely why Jesus took them upon himself. All of that is covered. And yet there are teachers who still reach into that old covenant and pull out whatever fits a particular agenda — political, social, financial. There are preachers who leverage the sincere faith of good people to extract money in exchange for miraculous outcomes. Please do not fall for it. That is not the gospel. It is a distortion of it, and it needs to stop.

Those first-century Christians were on something I can only describe as a supernatural spiritual highway. They had no media, no institutions, no political allies — and yet they turned the ancient world upside down. The cross and the resurrection had done something in them that reoriented their entire relationship to life and death. They existed simultaneously in two worlds: physically present on this earth, and spiritually at home in another. And once that became real to them, the Colosseum lost its power to terrify. Being fed to lions was not the end; it was simply the passage. That shift in perspective — from earthly thinking to the view from eternity — was the transformation that others saw and wanted for themselves. It is what Paul called the secret. And I believe it is still available. Could you look at a stage 4 diagnosis, a shattered marriage, a prodigal child, an untimely death — and find in it not despair, but the deep, settled peace of someone who knows whose they are and where they are headed?

You can say "I do" and never take the next step. That is your choice, and it will not cost you eternity. But the next step — the decision to actually walk with Jesus, to engage the faith lens, to build on rock — that is where the peace, the assurance, and the deep satisfaction that your soul is hungry for actually begin to take shape. Maybe life is going well right now. Maybe you are in a good season, everything is clicking, and this all feels a little academic. If that is you, I would gently say: this is exactly where the foolish man was. He did not think the storm was coming either. When something in your life eventually breaks — and something will — that is not a sign that God has failed you or that you have been singled out. It is simply the world being what it is. You were never meant to carry this world alone.

One of the most practical and powerful things you can do to find your footing on this road is to join a Bible study group. I know that may sound simple, even a little ordinary. But there is something that happens when you sit weekly with people who are honestly engaging the same questions — who will offer you accountability, share their own struggles, and help you understand what you are reading. They will help you activate the Spirit that is already in you, already reaching toward God, already nudging you in the right direction. You do not have to figure this out alone.

Let us return to Matthew 11, and hear it fresh:

- "Come to me all of you" — Jesus never made any restrictions on who should or should not come.
- "That are weary and are carrying heavy burdens" — that's you.
- "And I will give you rest" — the peace that comes from following.
- "Take my yoke upon you and learn from me" — follow me.
- "For I am gentle and humble in heart" — always forgives, never holds a grudge.
- "And you will find rest for your souls" — life satisfaction.
- "For my yoke is easy, and my burden is light" — following does not require you to give up who you are. Extrovert or introvert, you do not have to change to follow.

Is it possible for you to change direction? To follow Jesus into a different way of seeing, a different way of carrying the weight of your life? Maybe you have been letting the days go by long enough. Maybe it is time to take a new road. Follow him, and perhaps for the first time, really live.

CHAPTER 8
BUT IF NOT

"Our God whom we serve is able to deliver us from the fiery furnace, and he will deliver us out of thine hand, O king. **But if not**, let it be known unto thee, O king, that we will not serve thy gods, nor worship the golden image which thou hast set up. (Daniel 3:17-18)"

Most of us treat prayer like a vending machine — insert request, wait for delivery, feel cheated when nothing comes out. This chapter is going to dismantle that. Built around three words whispered from a desperate battlefield in World War II — words that trace all the way back to three men standing at the edge of a furnace — Chapter 8 takes on the question most people are too frustrated to ask honestly: what is prayer actually for? If God already knows what you need before you ask, why ask at all? The answer, it turns out, changes everything — not about God, but about you.

A Question for God

Three men stood at the edge of a furnace and said something that has echoed across twenty-six centuries. King Nebuchadnezzar had given Shadrach, Meshach, and Abednego a simple choice: bow to his golden idol, or burn. Their answer was not a negotiation, not a desperate bargain with God, and not a declaration of certainty about how things would turn out. It was something far rarer — a statement of complete surrender to whatever God allowed. They told the king directly: " Our God is able to deliver us from this furnace, and he may well do exactly that. ***But If Not*** — if this is where it ends for us — we are at peace with it. And either way, we will not bow."

But if not. Three words. They did not demand a miracle. They did not make their faith conditional on the outcome. They simply placed themselves in God's hands and held their ground.

Fast forward to May 1940. The beaches of Dunkirk, France, are packed with 350,000 British soldiers, pinned against the English Channel with the German army closing in behind them. Evacuation by conventional military means is nearly impossible. The situation is, by any military calculation, catastrophic. In the midst of it, a British naval officer sends a message back to London — not a tactical report, not a detailed rescue request. Just three words: ***But if not.***

In a London still deeply rooted in scripture, those three words landed with the full weight of their origin. People knew immediately what they meant — not just that the situation was desperate, but that the men on those beaches were surrendering the outcome to God while doing everything within their power to survive. What happened next is one of the most remarkable episodes of the Second World War. The Axis forces hesitated — inexplicably, given their overwhelming advantage. And in that window, an armada assembled itself out of nothing: naval destroyers alongside merchant vessels, pleasure cruisers, fishing boats, private yachts. Ordinary British civilians crossed the Channel in boats never designed for anything like this. Over nine days, more than 338,000 soldiers were brought home.

Whether you call it providence or coincidence, the parallel is impossible to ignore. Shadrach, Meshach, and Abednego walked out of the furnace. The soldiers walked off the beach. Neither outcome was guaranteed. Both groups had surrendered the result before they knew what it would be.

Which brings us to the prayer that both groups were really praying — the one that sits underneath all the specific requests we bring to God: *Oh God, what is your will?* It is the hardest prayer most of us will ever pray, because it requires letting go of the outcome before we know what it is. What is God's will for this marriage? For this diagnosis? For this child who has gone off the rails? For this addiction that will not release its grip?

Here is something worth being clear about, because churches have muddied this considerably: God's will is not a detailed itinerary for your life. He is not the author of a specific script that you must locate and follow precisely, or else miss your destiny. He did not pre-select your career, your spouse, the number of children you would have, or the city where you would live. The plan for your life — in those particulars — is genuinely yours to make. What God has a will about is something deeper and more consistent: how you live, how you treat people, what you do with what you have been given. It may be God's will that you use your particular gifts to serve others. But he is not going to tell you whether to be a dentist or an engineer, whether to live in Phoenix or Portland. Those are your choices, made within the larger frame of a life oriented toward him.

The distinction matters enormously. Confusing God's will with a specific life plan leads to paralysis — the fear of making the wrong choice and missing the path God intended. It also leads to the kind of false comfort that explains away tragedy: "this must have been God's plan." When something terrible happens, that is not God's plan expressing itself. That is the world being what it is. God's will is not the author of the furnace. It is the presence that meets you inside it.

Which Way?

Be honest for a moment. How many of your prayers have actually been answered the way you hoped? You prayed for the job and got it. You prayed for the test and passed. But then there were the other prayers — the ones that went nowhere, the silence that stretched on, the moment you finally stopped asking because it felt like no one was listening. And somewhere in that silence, a conclusion formed: God does not answer prayer. Maybe God does not care. Maybe God is not even there.

That conclusion is understandable. But it may be built on a flawed premise — that prayer is primarily a delivery mechanism. You place your order, God fulfills it, and the relationship is essentially transactional. When the orders stop coming through, the whole system loses its credibility.

But what if that is not what prayer is for?

Before Jesus taught his followers how to pray, he taught them how not to. And the common thread running through his examples of bad prayer is the same in every case: it is all about the person praying. The laundry list of requests thrown at the ceiling. The memorized scripture recited to impress. The repetitive phrases that have been drained of all meaning through sheer repetition. Jesus was not impressed by any of it — and he said so plainly. God already knows what you need before you open your mouth. So if he already knows, what exactly is the point of asking?

This is where the whole thing pivots. Jesus is not describing prayer as a way for you to move God. He is describing it as a way for God to move you.

Think about what that changes. If prayer is about submission rather than petition — about aligning yourself with what God is already doing rather than lobbying for what you want him to do —

then an unanswered prayer is not a failure of the system. It may be the system working exactly as intended, quietly repositioning your perspective rather than rearranging your circumstances.

That does not make it easy. When you are staring at a diagnosis, a broken marriage, a child in crisis, the last thing you want is perspective. You want results. I understand that. But the God Jesus describes is not a vending machine, and the prayer Jesus models is not a transaction. It is a conversation between a child and a father — one who already knows what you need and is far more interested in who you are becoming than in simply making your problems disappear.

So before we walk through the prayer Jesus actually taught, it is worth asking the question he seemed to want his followers to wrestle with: not "why isn't God answering?" but "what am I really asking for — and am I willing to let God answer in his own way?"

The Force of Will

Before you pray, stop. Find a quiet place — a room, a chair, a spot where you can close a door and leave the noise on the other side. This is not incidental advice. Jesus was deliberate about it. He said, "Go into your room, close the door, and pray to your Father in secret." Not in traffic. Not while half-watching television. Not in the thirty seconds before a meal when everyone is already thinking about the food. Those moments have their place, but they are not this. What follows requires your full attention, because you are about to address someone who deserves it.

Our Father in heaven.

Jesus instructs us to address God as Father. Not Judge. Not Scorekeeper. Not the distant cosmic authority who reviews your file with mounting disappointment. Father. It is the most intimate word in the prayer, and Jesus chose it deliberately. Some of you will find this easy. Others will find it loaded — because the word father carries weight that has nothing to do with God, and everything to do with the man who raised you, or didn't. If that is you, bring it. Bring the complication, the ambivalence, the wound. God is not fragile, and this prayer is not a performance.

Hallowed be your name.

This phrase gets skipped over so quickly that most people have no idea what it means. Hallowed simply means holy — set apart, beyond ordinary, unlike anything else. But pausing here is about more than vocabulary. It is about orientation. Before you bring your needs, your questions, your frustrations — before you get to any of that — you stop and acknowledge who you are actually talking to. A being beyond all comprehension, yet somehow capable of the most personal intimacy. That combination is staggering when you sit with it for a moment. The God who holds the universe together is the same God who invites you to close a door and speak to him privately. Taking that in before you say another word changes the posture of everything that follows.

Thy kingdom come, thy will be done.

And here is where most of us quietly check out. Because this is the line that bumps directly into everything we came to pray about. My kingdom. My will. My situation. The bills, the diagnosis, the relationship that is falling apart, the child who is breaking my heart. What about all of that?

Here is what Jesus is doing. He is not dismissing your needs — he already told you that God knows them before you ask. What he is doing is repositioning you. He is asking you to start the conversation not with your agenda, but with his. Not because your needs are unimportant, but because walking into prayer with your fist full of demands and your eyes fixed on outcomes tends to produce exactly the kind of transactional, vending-machine relationship that leaves you feeling unheard and God feeling like a service provider.

Praying "thy will be done" is not resignation. It is not giving up or pretending you do not want what you want. It is the act of opening your hands — saying, I have my hopes and my fears and my very specific requests, and I am laying them down in front of you, trusting that you see more than I do. It is the prayer of Shadrach, Meshach, and Abednego. It is the prayer cabled from the beach at Dunkirk. It is the hardest prayer in the book, and Jesus put it near the beginning on purpose.

Now, don't confuse God's will with the "plan for your life" that churches love to talk about. I can't find any place in the Bible where God promises to do this. God's will is not a job title, a zip code, or a five-year roadmap. He's not going to tell you which career to pick, who to marry, whether you should buy that car or boat, or whether to take the exit ramp on I-90. What he *is* doing — through Scripture, through the gentle nudges of the Spirit, through other people in your life — is shaping how you move through the world. His will shows up in the concrete and the everyday: being generous with your money, going out of your way for someone who's struggling, giving your time to something that matters, or simply changing the way you react in a situation where you'd normally blow it. Anything that bears the fruits of the Spirit — that's the territory of God's will.

What is keeping you from praying it? That is worth sitting with before you move on. If there is something in your life that you are not willing to surrender — a situation you are not willing to let God handle on his own terms — that resistance is almost certainly the most important thing you could bring into this room. Name it. Put it on the table. Tell God you are not sure you can let go of it yet. That is not a failure of faith. That is the beginning of an honest conversation.

Suppose you are having trouble with his will. Maybe you don't like or understand what God is doing or allowing to happen. If you are struggling with this, I suggest that you stop praying now and proceed to the section called "Show Me the Light."

On earth as it is in heaven.

Where is all of this supposed to happen? Not in some future state. Not after you die, or after things get better, or after you finally have enough margin in your life to be generous. Here. Now. In your home, your marriage, your workplace, your neighborhood. In the way you speak to the person who irritates you most. In the choice you make when no one is watching. In the quiet decision to be a little more patient, a little more honest, a little more present than you were yesterday.

This is where God's will lands — not in the abstract, but in the specific texture of an ordinary Tuesday. And the question Jesus is quietly asking is the same one I find myself asking when I pray this line: what is actually keeping me from doing it?

Rescue

The prayer shifts here. Everything up to this point has been about orientation — acknowledging who God is, surrendering your agenda, aligning yourself with his will. Now it becomes personal. This is where you bring your actual life into the room.

Give us today our daily bread.

Notice the word daily. Not annually. Not a lump sum provision that covers everything in advance, so you never have to ask again. Daily. One day at a time. There is something intentional in that — a built-in reminder that dependence on God is not a one-time transaction but an ongoing posture. The things we most desperately need are almost always the things we have the least control over. Will this treatment work? Will my child be okay? Will I make it through this season financially? Will the loneliness lift? These are not things you can engineer or willpower your way through. They are the places where, whether you acknowledge it or not, you are already dependent. This line makes that dependence honest.

Forgive us our debts, as we forgive our debtors.

This one has teeth. God forgives me — and at the same time, I forgive the people who have wronged me. The two move together. Not sequentially, not conditionally, but simultaneously. Which means that asking God to forgive you while you are quietly refusing to forgive someone else is a contradiction that does not go unnoticed. It is the spiritual equivalent of asking God to clean your slate while you hold someone else's hostage.

This is not about making a list of your sins and reciting them. If you have said "I do believe," the forgiveness is already done — the cross took care of that. What this line really asks for is help. Help to extend to others what has already been extended to you. The prayer might sound something like: God, thank you for forgiving me. Now give me the strength to forgive them — because on my own, I am not sure I can. That is an honest prayer. That is one God can work with.

And lead us not into temptation, but deliver us from evil.

This is a rescue call. Plain and simple. Evil does not typically announce itself — it rarely shows up looking like what it is. It shows up looking like relief, or excitement, or something you deserve after a hard week. The flirtation that feels harmless. The app that seems like just a bit of fun. The first drink that does not feel like the beginning of anything. By the time it looks like what it actually is, you are often already inside it.

That is why this line comes before the fall, not after. You are not asking God to clean up a mess that has already happened. You are asking him to intervene before it does — to prompt you, to redirect you, to make the exit visible before you have gone too far to use it.

But here is where it gets complicated. If the temptation is not something that found you, but something you went looking for — if there is a pattern of planning and then asking for forgiveness, planning and then asking for forgiveness — this prayer cannot be used to cover that cycle indefinitely. You cannot consciously engineer a situation and then ask God to deliver you from the consequences of your own design. That is not prayer. That is manipulation. And a God beyond all comprehension is not fooled by it.

What the prayer is actually inviting, in those cases, is something harder and more honest: God, why do I keep going back to this? What am I actually looking for? What am I afraid of? What emptiness am I trying to fill? Those are the questions underneath the pattern, and they are the ones worth bringing into this room — not to perform repentance, but to actually get to the root of something that keeps pulling you off course.

The temptation wheel — gratify yourself, protect yourself, live for yourself, then feel worse about yourself — spins until something stops it. This prayer is the brake. Without it, the wheel keeps going, and the "help me" prayer you make when everything falls apart becomes inevitable. With it, you can slow down before you get there.

When the Door Opens

When you have finished, open the door. Continue praying — for the people you love, for those who are suffering, for your country, for the situations that weigh on you. Pray for those who make it easy, and for those who do not. This part of the prayer is expansive and generous, and it is where the orientation you established at the beginning of the prayer starts to express itself outward. You came in focused on yourself. You go out focused on others. That movement — inward to outward, receiving to giving — is not accidental. It is the shape of a life that is growing in the right direction.

Shed some light

There are seasons when the standard prayer will not come. You sit down, you close the door, you try to begin — and nothing moves. Not because you have stopped believing, but because something in you is stuck. You are wrestling with what God is allowing. You are angry about what he has not done. You are confused by the silence, or exhausted by a situation that prayer does not seem to be touching. In those moments, forcing your way through the Our Father can feel hollow — words without weight, form without feeling.

If that is where you are, Jesus has something for you. And it comes in the form of a story about a blind man on the side of a road.

His name was Bartimaeus. He sat where he always sat, begging at the roadside outside Jericho, when he heard an unusual commotion. A crowd was moving through, and at its center was Jesus of Nazareth. Bartimaeus had heard enough about Jesus to know that this was a moment he could not afford to miss. So he did the only thing he could think of — he started shouting. "Jesus, Son of David, have mercy on me!"

The crowd told him to be quiet. He was an embarrassment, a disruption, an inconvenience to people who were trying to listen to something important. He shouted louder. "Son of David, have mercy on me!" He was not going to be silenced by people who could already see.

Jesus stopped. In a crowd of followers, with teaching to be done and a city ahead, he stopped — because one desperate, undignified voice had cut through everything else. He asked that Bartimaeus be brought to him, and then he asked him a question that must have struck the crowd as almost absurd: "What do you want me to do for you?"

It seems obvious, doesn't it? He's blind. But Jesus asked anyway. And there is something important in that. Jesus does not assume. He does not project onto you what he thinks you need. He asks. And he waits for you to say it out loud, specifically, honestly — not because he doesn't already know, but because there is something that happens in the naming of it. Something that moves in you when you stop hinting and start asking directly.

Bartimaeus did not hedge. He did not say, "Well, whatever your will is" — not because surrendering to God's will was wrong, but because he had a specific, honest request and he was going to make it. "I want to see." Three words. No preamble, no apology, no theological qualification. Just the truth of what he needed.

"Receive your sight. Your faith has healed you."

And then Bartimaeus did something the story makes easy to overlook. He followed Jesus. Not back to his spot on the roadside, not home to tell his family — he followed Jesus into Jerusalem. Which means he was there for everything that came next. The triumphal entry. The temple. The arrest. The trial. The crucifixion. The man who had been given his sight watched the one who gave it to him die on a cross. And he stayed.

That is what it looks like to receive something from Jesus and then follow him into the hard places rather than retreating to the comfortable ones.

So if you are stuck — if the Our Father feels out of reach today, if you are struggling to submit to a will you do not currently understand, if you are angry or confused or worn out — try this prayer instead, not as a replacement, but as a doorway.

Lord, I want to see.

Help me see this marriage the way you see it. Help me see this diagnosis — mine, or someone I love — the way you see it. Help me see the person I cannot forgive, the situation I cannot accept, and the outcome I am terrified of, through your eyes, rather than mine. Help me see why this is happening, or help me make peace with not knowing why. Help me see what you are doing in this, even when I cannot feel it.

It is a dangerous prayer, in the best possible sense. Because seeing often requires something of you, it may mean letting go of a position you have held for years. It may require you to extend grace to someone who has not asked for it. It may require you to admit that the way you have been seeing a situation has been wrong, or incomplete, or shaped more by your own wounds than by anything resembling truth. Seeing can be uncomfortable. It can cost you the familiar darkness you have learned to navigate, in exchange for a light that shows you things you were not sure you wanted to look at.

But it is the prayer Jesus answered for Bartimaeus without hesitation. And it is the prayer he is still answering — for anyone willing to stop by the side of the road, let go of their dignity for a moment, and ask for it directly.

When you are ready to see, ask. And then, like Bartimaeus, be willing to follow where the answer leads.

CHAPTER 9

WHAT WILL YOUR VERSE BE?

Oh me! Oh life! of the questions of these recurring,
Of the endless trains of the faithless, of cities fill'd with the foolish,
Of myself forever reproaching myself, (for who more foolish than I, and who more faithless?)
Of eyes that vainly crave the light, of the objects mean, of the struggle ever renew'd,
Of the poor results of all, of the plodding and sordid crowds I see around me,
Of the empty and useless years of the rest, with the rest me intertwined,
The question, O me! so sad, recurring—What good amid these, O me, O life?

Answer.

*That you are here—that life exists and **Identity**,*
*That **The Powerful Play** goes on, and you may contribute a **Verse.***

O Me! O Life
by Walt Whitman

What will your verse be?

This chapter is about purpose. Not the vague, inspirational kind — not a poster on a wall or a mission statement in a drawer — but the real kind, the kind that gives a life its shape and its meaning. It is about why you are here, what you were made for, and what stands between you and actually living it. It is also about the thing Jesus called losing your life in order to find it — one of the most counterintuitive ideas he ever offered, and one of the most true. If you have ever had the quiet sense that there must be more to your life than what you've been filling it with, this chapter is for you.

The Powerful Play

Why would a good and loving God allow bad things to happen? It is the oldest question in the book — and it deserves a serious answer. But before we get there, I want to turn it around for a moment. Why would a good and loving God allow *you* to happen?

Think about the last seven days. Not your highlight reel — the actual week. The lie you told because the truth was inconvenient. The person you hurt and did not apologize to. The jealousy that quietly poisoned something good. The anger that came out sideways at someone who did not deserve it. The thing you put ahead of God, ahead of the people you love, ahead of your own better judgment. The gossip. The grudge. The moment you knew the right thing to do and chose something else anyway.

We are very good at cataloging the evil in the world and very slow to account for our own contribution to it. Before we ask why God allows suffering, it is worth sitting with the fact that we are part of what God is allowing — and he allows us anyway.

Here is the story as simply as it can be told. There was a time when things were whole — when the trust between God and the people he made was intact, and the world reflected that. Then that trust broke.

Humanity decided, in its very first act of genuine freedom, that God could not be trusted — that his instructions were a constraint rather than a gift, and that going a different direction would lead somewhere better. It did not. When that break happened, something entered the world that was never part of the original design: evil, with everything it carries — sickness, death, sorrow, the long accumulation of damage that human beings do to each other and to themselves.

And into that broken world, a light stepped. Not to wave a hand and make the darkness disappear, but to enter it — fully, in the flesh, without using his divine advantage to sidestep any of it. As John writes, the light shines in the darkness, and the darkness has not overcome it. Jesus did not begin by eliminating evil from the world. He began by addressing it in the only place he had direct access to: individual human hearts, one at a time, including mine. He took the evil in me upon himself and settled the account — so that when God looks at me, he does not see what I actually am without Jesus. He sees what Jesus has made me. That is not a small thing. And it means that no religion, no person, no voice in your own head has the right to define you as irredeemably broken. In Christ, that verdict has been overturned.

This is what I call the Powerful Play — the ongoing drama of good and evil that every human being alive is caught up in, whether they acknowledge it or not. It is not a metaphor. It is the actual shape of history, of every news cycle, of every personal crisis, of every moment of unexpected beauty or devastating loss. We live in a world where good and evil genuinely coexist, where both are real, and where what we choose to do with our freedom genuinely matters.

If the world contained only good, there would be no Powerful Play — and no role for you in it. Your choices would be irrelevant because the outcome would already be fixed. If the world contained only evil, the Play would be over — there would be nothing left worth fighting for. It is precisely because both exist, in tension, that your life has actual stakes. One day, Jesus will return and end the conflict permanently. But not yet. Right now, the Play is still running, and you have a part in it whether you have claimed it or not.

The question of why God allows evil at all does not have a simple answer. But it helps to make a distinction that often gets overlooked. There are two kinds of evil in the Powerful Play.

The first is moral evil — the damage human beings deliberately inflict on each other. Betrayal, violence, corruption, cruelty, the thousand quieter forms of harm we do when we choose ourselves over everyone else. This kind of evil has a clear origin: human freedom, misused. God did not create it. We did, with the freedom he gave us, in the moment we decided we knew better.

The second is natural evil — cancer, earthquakes, pandemics, the random disasters that arrive without warning and without moral logic. A child born with a degenerative disease. A community destroyed by a flood. A perfectly healthy person who gets a diagnosis that changes everything on an ordinary Tuesday. This kind of evil is harder to account for, and it elicits two very different responses depending on where you stand.

The observer — the person watching someone else suffer — tends to ask intellectual questions. How could a good God allow this? The questions are legitimate. But they can also become a reason to step back from faith entirely, concluding that a God who permits this kind of suffering is either absent, indifferent, or fictional. Richard Dawkins put the atheist position plainly: the universe has precisely the properties we should expect if there is no design, no purpose, no good and no evil — nothing but blind, pitiless indifference.

I understand the appeal of that position. It is internally consistent. But it carries a cost that Dawkins does not fully reckon with. If there is no good and no evil — if those are simply human constructs with no grounding in anything real — then why does injustice make us furious? Why do we build hospitals? Why do we risk our lives for strangers? Why does the evening news produce outrage rather than indifference? The sense of moral obligation — the deep, inarticulate conviction that some things are wrong and must be resisted — is not easily explained by a universe of blind indifference. Where does it come from? Why is it etched so deeply into people who have never read a word of scripture? And more importantly, who put it there?

The victim — the person inside the suffering rather than watching from outside it — tends to ask a different question. Not "how could God allow this?" but "where is God in this?" And that is where Christianity speaks most directly, because Christianity does not offer the suffering person a philosophical argument. It offers them a presence. A God who entered the suffering himself, who knows what it is to be abandoned and in pain, who promises that the story does not end here. You cannot go through this world on brutal reality alone. At some point, hope is not a luxury — it is the only thing left for that suffering person. And the question is whether the hope you are holding is built on something real.

You cannot change the Powerful Play. There will always be injustice. There will always be disease and disaster, and the particular cruelty of people who have decided that their own interests are the only ones that matter. That is not going to be fixed by better politics, more awareness, or any human program, however well-intentioned.

But that does not mean you are a spectator. The Powerful Play needs actors — people who have been changed from the inside out and are willing to take that change into the world. People who sit with the suffering rather than explain it. People who show up where the damage is worst and do what they can with what they have. People whose transformation is visible enough that others ask what happened to them.

Maybe it starts with you. Maybe the most powerful argument

for the existence of a good God is not a philosophical proof but a transformed life — someone who should, by all accounts, be bitter or broken, but isn't. Someone who has found something real enough to build on, solid enough to hold when the storms come, and generous enough to share.

That is your verse in the Powerful Play. And it is worth showing up to claim it.

Identity

Default Settings

You were created for a purpose in the Powerful Play. Your identity is the gateway to finding it. But before you can find it, you need to confront something uncomfortable: the operating system you've been running on your whole life.

David Foster Wallace called it your "default setting." It's the factory-installed belief that you are the center of the world and everyone else is just in the way. It runs quietly, constantly — and most of us never notice it.

Here's what it looks like. The guy at the gym hogging the equipment is a dope. The woman on the subway — why doesn't she take better care of herself? The banged-up car weaving through traffic — that guy is clearly a mess. You don't say any of this out loud. You don't have to. The default setting doesn't need permission. It just runs.

And before you say "that's not me" — take a breath. The default setting doesn't announce itself as selfishness. It disguises itself as common sense, as having standards, as simply knowing how things should work. Good people run on default settings. Generous people do too. People who genuinely believe they are kind and thoughtful still wake up every morning and, without thinking, place themselves at the center of the story. That's what makes it a default — you don't have to think.

When the default setting stops being just a mood and hardens into who you are, ideology moves in. And this is where things get genuinely dangerous.

When your identity fuses with a belief system — political, social, religious — something fundamental shifts, a challenge to your ideas no longer feels like a disagreement. It feels like an attack on *you*, personally. And that distinction changes everything, because now you are no longer defending a position — you are defending yourself. The walls go up. The drawbridge comes down.

People on the far left and far right both know this feeling, even if neither would admit it. Someone deep in either camp has stopped being curious. They already know. And people who already know everything have quietly stopped growing. The details of the ideology differ; the mechanism is identical.

What follows is almost mechanical. You find your tribe — the people who use the same words, share the same outrage, and applaud at exactly the right moments. The bubble forms not from weakness but from the relief of being understood, of never having to defend the obvious. And once you are inside it, the bubble must be protected at all costs — even when logic runs counter to it, even when the statistics don't cooperate, even when a reasonable person from the outside could dismantle the whole thing in ten minutes. Facts stop mattering. They become inconvenient rather than instructive. You don't update your beliefs — you harden them.

The most dangerous part is what you lose without noticing: intellectual curiosity. The habit of asking *what if I'm wrong?* The willingness to sit with a question longer than it takes to find a confirming answer. The person who was once genuinely open gradually becomes someone who performs openness while doing nothing of the kind. They're not lying, exactly. They've just forgotten what curiosity felt like. The bubble became a personality, and the personality became a cage — comfortable, familiar, and entirely of their own making.

Christians aren't immune to this either. It's ironic — and worth sitting with — that some who follow Jesus use him as justification for judging others, overturning tables, drawing hard lines. But Jesus never said, "Do what I did." He said, "Follow me." He knew that any attempt to replicate his actions without his nature would produce the opposite effect. That's why he taught in parables. He wasn't saying, "Hey, watch this." He was pointing to something deeper.

The default setting, or an identity fused with ideology, isn't just a bad habit. It's a trap. And the world has no interest in helping you out of it — because the world runs on default settings and broken ideologies. It's the whole business model.

The Holy Spirit wants to give you something different: a new identity, a new center, a new set of settings. But here's the catch — you can't run both operating systems at once and expect to get anywhere. Something has to give. And what has to give, it turns out, is the belief that you were ever meant to be the center of the story in the first place.

That's not the end of your identity. It's the beginning of it.

Time for a change

Changing your default setting is the threshold to finding your identity. But it doesn't happen automatically or overnight. It starts with a single, uncomfortable shift: maybe this isn't about me.

Remember those people? The guy at the gym who can't seem to get off the equipment — he's been staring at his phone because the layoffs at his company were just announced, and his mind is somewhere else entirely. The woman on the subway you silently judged — she has an anxiety disorder, and the medication keeping her functional is also the reason she's gained weight. She'd love to work out. But she's a single mom who has to get home, get the kids to bed, and get ready to do it all again tomorrow. The guy in the banged-up car driving like his hair is on fire — he's late for his second job, the one that pays for his five-year-old son's chemotherapy.

You didn't know any of that. Neither did I. That's the point.

This isn't a guilt trip. Not every stranger carries a hidden tragedy. But in the Powerful Play, these are not just possible — they are someone's actual reality, happening right now, all around you. The default setting never stops to consider that. It just renders its verdict and moves on.

Stepping back from that verdict — pausing before the judgment, choosing curiosity over contempt — is what it looks like to move off your default settings, and maybe removing yourself from the ideology. And yes, it's harder than it sounds. It disrupts the efficient, self-contained rhythm of your day. It costs something. Paying attention to people you don't know, extending empathy to strangers who haven't earned it, making someone else's problem worth a moment of your time — none of that comes naturally. The default setting was designed for speed, not depth. Being able to look at a news story or situation not the way the herd does, but by asking the right questions and studying the facts, will help you break free from the clutches of your ideology.

But here's what changes everything. You don't have to manufacture this on willpower alone. The cross isn't just a symbol of forgiveness — it's the source of momentum. When you truly grasp that your guilt has been erased, that you are free, that nothing you've done is being held over you — something opens up. You stop spending so much energy defending yourself, managing your image, protecting your place at the center, or treating a left-wing or right-wing ideology like it is some faith-based religion.

And in that freed-up space, something else becomes possible: you can actually see the people around you.

That's the work of the Holy Spirit. Not a feeling, not a mood — a genuine reorientation of your attention. It moves you from the exhausting project of keeping yourself at the center to the far more interesting project of figuring out who you actually are and what you were put here to do.

Your identity is not something you construct. It's something you discover — and it is always God's will, through prayer and through surrender, that you find it.

Jesus Steps In

The world and Christianity are fundamentally at odds on this one thing: your identity. The world wants you operating on your default settings — consuming, competing, accumulating, performing. The Holy Spirit wants to give you something entirely different. The problem is you can't run both at once and expect to get anywhere meaningful.

As I stated above and will state again to drive it home, trying to operate without your default settings is genuinely hard. It interrupts the flow of an already demanding day. That report is due to your boss, the year-end inventory, the relentless logistics of getting kids from one place to the next — all of it pressing in, all of it screaming that you are the most important variable in the equation. Stepping off that throne, even briefly, feels unnatural. Because it is. The default setting has been honed over years of practice.

It's just easier to operate in the default setting to pursue satisfaction than to change: more tasks, more things, more experiences, more toys.

And there's always a rationale — I worked hard for this, I deserve it, I'm being a good steward. But underneath the rationale is something closer to fear. Fear that without all of it, there isn't enough of you. That the empty feeling at the center won't go away on its own. That if you stop accumulating, stop performing, stop filling — you might discover there's nothing there.

That fear is not an accident. When evil entered the world, it didn't just bring death, disease, and malice. It took you from you. It handed you a counterfeit identity and told you it was the real thing. It plugged you into a belief system where your hope becomes the unwritten documents of the ideology. And the world has been reinforcing that lie ever since — through every commercial, every social media feed, every quiet cultural message that says your value is in what you have and what you've achieved. It has been enforcing it through every slanted news channel you watch. The real you is still in there somewhere. But the world needs you not to find it.

Jesus knew exactly what had been done to you. And he wasn't interested in helping you manage it better. He came to recover it entirely.

In Mark 8:34, he puts it this way:

"If any wish to come after me, let them deny themselves, take up their cross and follow me."

That word "deny" is doing a lot of work. It doesn't mean self-punishment or joyless living. It means saying no to the counterfeit — the false self the world handed you — so the real one has room to emerge. And the cross, in the first century, wasn't a piece of jewelry. If you were carrying one, everyone knew you had surrendered your so-called freedom. Jesus is saying: that freedom you've been white-knuckling? It's an ankle bracelet. It was never freedom at all.

Then Jesus continues in Mark 8:

"For those who want to save their life will lose it, and those who lose their life for my sake, and for the sake of the gospel, will save it. For what will it profit them to gain the whole world and forfeit their life?"

The Greek word translated as "lose" here doesn't mean death. It means to lose out — to ruin something by trying too hard to control it. Think about making a pizza. You start with a great recipe, but you keep tweaking it — a little more of this, a little less of that — until somewhere along the way it loses its flavor entirely. You ruined it by refusing to leave it alone. That's what happens when you try to save your life on your own terms. You grip it so tightly, curate it so carefully, that it slips through your fingers anyway. You let the days go by. And one day you look up and feel an emptiness you can't explain, having spent years filling yourself with things that were never going to work.

This isn't a small problem. Look around. The rates of depression, anxiety, addiction, and suicide are not the result of people having too little. They are the result of people desperately searching for an identity in places that cannot provide one—and coming up empty-handed again and again. The things the world sells are not without value. Good food, real beauty, love, laughter — these matter. But they were never meant to be the answer to the deepest question: showing love, having romance, beauty, helping and encouraging others, being kind to those not as fortunate as you, having empathy, sympathy, bearing all the fruits of the spirit that we talked about before – this is what we stay alive for.

Doing these things unlocks your identity — and, it turns out, your identity is not about accumulation. It's about scattering.

Losing your life isn't martyrdom. It's more like planting. You take the parts of yourself — your time, your talent, your treasure — and you scatter them like seeds across the Powerful Play. Jesus says that losing your life is a decision, a choice you make. And that slightly mistranslated phrase, "for my sake"? He doesn't mean live your life *for* him in some performative, religious sense. He means emulate the way he lived. Follow his lead. If you do that, you're essentially living for him — but it comes from the inside out, not the other way around.

And let's be clear about one thing: this is not what gets you into heaven. Only faith does that. This is something else entirely. This is identity. This is what you were made for.

Look at the cross. He chose to give up his life and scatter it across the world — freely, without condition. The fact that I'm writing this book and you're sitting there reading it is a testament to how far those seeds have traveled.

So that's who we are. We live like Christ, and in doing so, we reflect him. We don't put a bowl over the light — we let it shine. Not so people will notice us, but so they can actually see something. This is your design. Not to shop, not to climb, not to collect degrees or build an impressive portfolio of stuff. Those things aren't your identity. They're furniture.

Here's what brings it home: when you truly understand what God has done for you — when it sinks in that he genuinely has your best interests at heart and that his love for you is real — something shifts. You stop asking what's in it for you and start asking what you can do for someone else because that's what was done for you.

And if you can do that? You've saved your life.

Think about it this way. The people who seem to have it all together — the ones who project confidence and success and self-sufficiency — are often the most hollow. Meanwhile, your biggest regrets, the moments you'd go back and undo if you could, were almost certainly the moments when it was all about you. You know the ones.

Now think about the opposite. Is there someone from your past — a teacher, a coach, a parent, a friend — who changed the course of your life simply by making time for you? They shared something, invested something, and it stuck. They made it about *you*, not about them. That's the seed. That's the scatter. That's the Powerful Play in action.

C.S. Lewis understood this. In *The Screwtape Letters*, he imagines a senior demon coaching a junior one on the single thing they must never allow a human being to discover: that surrendering yourself to God does not erase you — it restores you. The demon knows, with something like dread, that a person who genuinely steps off their default settings and gives themselves over to God will not become less of a person. They will become more themselves than they have ever been. That is the threat. That is what the demons are working to prevent.

Which means the very thing the world tells you will erase you — surrender, denying yourself, following Jesus — is actually the thing that gives you back to yourself. The self-will you have been clutching so tightly was never the real you. It was a cage dressed up as freedom. What God gives back, once you let go of it, is something deeper and truer: not a diminished version, not a religious performance, but the actual person he made — recovered from everything the world did to bury it.

The cross on the high steeple isn't just a religious symbol. It's a picture of the only journey that actually leads somewhere — the journey of losing the false self and becoming who you were always meant to be. That's where your verse begins. That's where everything changes.

The Verse

Let me start with a question the Beatles buried inside one of their more obscure songs, "Baby, You're a Rich Man." Strip away the melody, and you get this: *How does it feel to be one of the beautiful people? Now that you know who you are, what do you want to be?*

That last line is the one that gets me. Not what do you want to *do* for a living. Not what title do you want on a business card. What do you want to *be*?

Here's what I'm getting at. Your identity in Christ isn't a bumper sticker — it's supposed to reshape how you show up in every room you walk into. The bartender who makes a great drink *and* actually sees the guy at the end of the bar who's trying to drink his pain away. The nurse who's overworked and exhausted but still finds thirty seconds to look a scared patient in the eye and say, "I've got you." The accountant, the teacher, the truck driver, the stay-at-home parent — can you bring something different to the role now that you know who you are?

The Trap: Happy vs. Meaningful

Here's the rub — and this is one most people never figure out until it's too late.

Living a happy life is not the same as living a meaningful life. You can absolutely lead a meaningful life *and* be happy, but flip it around, and it rarely works. Happiness is mostly about what the world gives *to* you. Meaning is about what you give *out*. And the Powerful Play — that relentless machine we talked about in Chapter 2 — is only interested in keeping you chasing the former. As I said in previous chapters, leading a meaningful life is the key to satisfaction, not necessarily to happiness.

Jesus called this trap by its Greek name: *pleonexia*. Most of us translate it as "greed," and we immediately picture someone else — the greedy politician, the greedy ex, the greedy boss. Never ourselves. But that's exactly how pleonexia works. It doesn't show up wearing a villain's mask. It shows up disguised as common sense.

I work hard. I deserve this. I'm just being responsible — I need a reliable car, a bigger house, a better neighborhood. I'll be generous once I'm more settled.

Jesus walks into Luke 12, and someone in the crowd shouts, "Tell my brother to split the inheritance with me!" Jesus doesn't take the bait. He pivots — and what he says next is one of the most uncomfortable passages in all four Gospels:

"Take care! Be on your guard against all kinds of greed, for one's life does not consist in the abundance of possessions."

Then he tells the story of a wealthy farmer whose land produces a bumper crop. The man's response? Tear down the old barns, build bigger ones, store everything up. "Soul, you have ample goods laid up for many years; relax, eat, drink, be merry." God's response? *You fool. This very night, your life is being demanded of you. And the things you have prepared — whose will they be?"*

The farmer isn't condemned for *owning* things. He's condemned for being *owned* by them. For letting his net worth become his identity and his stockpile become his plan. His heirs won't remember the quality of his character. They're going to fight over the contents of his estate.

The insidious part of pleonexia is how it delays you. It whispers that the meaningful life starts *later* — after the kids are through college, after the mortgage is paid off, after you hit that number in the retirement account. But God peers into the Powerful Play and says, "You fool. Tonight." Not because he's cruel — but because later is a fiction we sell ourselves, and the clock is always running.

What Being "Rich Toward God" Actually Means

Here's where it gets good.

Jesus uses the phrase "rich toward God" at the end of the parable, and churches love to use that as a fundraising hook. But being rich toward God has nothing to do with your checkbook. God doesn't need your money. He created everything.

Being rich toward God means this: taking everything Christ has done for you and scattering it into other people's lives.

When you were lost, he came looking for you. When you needed forgiveness, he gave it without a bill attached. When you were on the wrong road, he put someone in your path who redirected you. When you were sick or broke or barely holding it together, he surrounded you with the right people at the right moment. *That* is what you're supposed to do for someone else.

Not from a distance. Not by writing a check to a cause you read about online. In the room, in the conversation, in the inconvenient moment when someone actually needs you.

When you live that way — when you stop being an end in yourself and start being a means to an end for someone else — something remarkable happens. It ripples. The person whose life you changed goes on to change someone else's, and they change someone else's, until the atomic force of what Christ set in motion bounces through generations of people you'll never meet. You won't be able to measure it. You won't get a notification about it. But it will last long after your 401(k) is someone else's argument.

One day, this will all end. That's not morbid — it's just true. The question is what shape your story has when it does.

A life spent accumulating will sift through your fingers like sand. But a life spent as a genuine instrument of grace in the people around you? That echoes. That's what gets remembered. That's what Jesus meant by "your verse."

Whether you're rich or broke, healthy or sick, employed or in the middle of a crisis, you can still have a verse. The Powerful Play doesn't require perfect circumstances. It requires a decision.

You were made for this. Now be it.

CHAPTER 10
STATION NOT DESTINATION

What if they were blessed for what they are doing in the world instead of chastened for not doing more at church? What if church felt more like a way station than a destination? — Barbara Brown Taylor, Leaving Church: A Memoir of Faith

Dysfunctional Destination

Let me say something that might surprise you, coming from a guy who just spent nine chapters talking about Jesus: you don't have to go to church.

There. I said it.

Now, before you close the book — I'm not telling you to stay home. If you've found a community where your soul genuinely connects to God and to the people around you, don't you dare leave over anything I write here. What I *am* saying is that "going to church" and "following Jesus" are not the same thing, and for millions of people, confusing the two has been quietly devastating to their faith.

But you should gather with other Christians – in homes, libraries, coffee shops, etc.

Here's where it started. After the resurrection, the Holy Spirit showed up at Pentecost, and the early followers of Jesus began meeting — not in buildings, not under a brand, but in each other's living rooms. Small gatherings. Shared meals. Real conversation about what Jesus actually said and did. The mission was simple: help each other grow, then go out and bring others in. That was it. No fog machines. No capital campaigns. No tier-one donor brunches—just people, trying to figure out how to follow someone who changed everything.

We've drifted a long way from that.

What the Numbers Say

This isn't just my opinion — the data is pretty clear. According to Gallup, about 30% of Americans attend religious services weekly or nearly weekly. Two decades ago, that number was 42%. A decade ago, it was 38%. That's not a blip; that's a trend with a direction. The Barna Group puts it even more bluntly: 33% of Americans are officially "de-churched" — meaning they used to attend, were actively involved, and walked away—one in three.

If Christianity were a company with those numbers, the board would have already fired the executive team. But churches don't have boards with teeth, and so the slide continues.

Something is clearly broken. The question worth asking isn't just *what* — it's *why*.

What a Church Is Supposed to Be

Before we diagnose the problem, let's be honest about what a church is actually for.

A church is supposed to be a gathering that produces disciples — people who know Jesus well enough to help someone else know him too. It's meant to help you forge your identity in Christ, find your verse in the Powerful Play, and send you *out* into the world equipped to do something with it. The church is not a building. It's not a stage, a bookstore, a coffee shop, or a childcare center. Those things aren't evil — but they're not the church. They're the furniture. And somewhere along the way, we started mistaking the furniture for the house.

What we have now is what I'd call the "church destination" — a place you go to, consume something, and go home. Like a restaurant, except the menu hasn't changed in decades and nobody's checking whether you're actually getting fed.

I want to be careful here, because this isn't a blanket indictment of everyone sitting in a pew or standing behind a pulpit. There are pastors doing extraordinary work. There are churches quietly feeding the hungry, housing the homeless, and genuinely discipling their people without any fanfare. I've met them. They exist. This critique isn't aimed at them — it's aimed at a *system* that has made their work harder, not easier.

How the System Went Sideways

For the sake of discussion, I've loosely grouped most Christian denominations into four buckets. The Mega Evangelical churches — "Megas." The mainline Protestant churches — Presbyterian, Lutheran, Methodist, Episcopal, Baptist, United Church of Christ, Reformed — which I'll call "PLUMBERS" (yes, that's intentional). The Pentecostal churches — "Pentys." And the Prosperity Gospel churches, which I'll simply call what they are: "Fools."

I've attended three churches in my life — Catholic, Mega, and Episcopal. None of them left me with a faith that was deeper than when I arrived. I've since learned that this experience isn't unusual. Most of the seasoned Christians I've spoken with over the years could tell you something similar: they showed up hungry, got entertained, and left the same.

Social media has cracked this open in a way that would have been impossible a generation ago. Pastors who preached grace on Sunday and operated with stunning hypocrisy Monday through Saturday are now being documented in real time. Authors, podcasters, filmmakers, and yes — even comedians — have done more to expose the gap between what churches claim to be and what they actually are than most denominational oversight bodies have managed in decades. It's uncomfortable. It's also long overdue.

The core problem isn't that churches have buildings or budgets or programs. Organizations need structure to function. The problem is when the structure becomes the point — when keeping the institution alive takes priority over the mission it was built to serve. That's the moment a church stops being a gathering and becomes a corporation. And corporations, by nature, optimize for survival and growth. They don't naturally optimize for your soul.

When the gathering becomes a corporation, the shift is subtle at first. The Sunday experience gets polished. The welcome process gets systematized. The giving talk gets more sophisticated. None of those things are inherently wrong. But over time, the metrics that matter start to change. Success is measured in campuses, attendance numbers, and square footage—not in whether people are actually being transformed or whether they could articulate the gospel to their next-door neighbor if asked.

The result is a Christianity that produces excellent church *consumers* and very few genuine disciples.

A Different Model

Here's what I keep coming back to: what if the first-century model wasn't primitive — what if it was just *right*?

Small gatherings. Genuine accountability. Leaders who were close enough actually to know the people they were shepherding. A mission that pointed *outward* rather than folding back inward to serve the institution. Churches that functioned less like destinations and more like launching pads.

What if church felt more like a way station than a final stop? What if the whole point was to move you *out* the door — better equipped, more rooted, more alive — rather than to keep you coming back to the show?

I'm not naïve enough to think the institution disappears overnight, or that it should. But I do think the Christians sitting in those pews deserve better than they're getting. They deserve leaders who measure their success not by how many people walked in the door, but by how many walked out changed. They deserve a gathering that's genuinely interested in helping them find their verse — not just filling a slot in a ministry roster.

That's the church worth building. And in the next section, we're going to talk about what it could actually look like. The question I have for Churches is a simple one: if we took away your building and your special programs, if we dissolved your corporation, would you still exist?

The Feudal Church

Today's church is a Feudal system invented at the dawn of a Feudal society and has never really deviated from this paradigm. Not metaphorically. *Structurally.*

The castle is the church building. The king is the pastor. The lords and ladies are the elders and deacons — loyal to the crown, insulated from any real accountability, and primarily useful for giving the congregation the *impression* that checks and balances exist. And you? You're the peasant. You show up, you tithe, you serve in an approved ministry, and you don't ask too many questions. The feudal church is your Sunday destination, and like any good feudal arrangement, the whole system is designed to funnel resources upward and keep the king on the throne.

This isn't an accident. It's a model that calcified over centuries, and most churches — even the ones with contemporary branding and a killer worship band — have never actually left it.

The King Has No Performance Review

Here's something that should bother you more than it probably does: being a pastor is one of the only leadership positions in modern America with virtually zero accountability.

No annual performance review. No board with the authority to remove them. No transparent financial reporting to the congregation that funds them. Protestant pastors are rarely fired — and when misconduct surfaces in Catholic churches, the response has historically been reassignment, not removal. The institution protects itself first. It always has.

I watched this play out firsthand at an Episcopal church I attended. One Sunday, without any scriptural basis whatsoever, the pastor informed us that not only would we have jobs in heaven, but we'd be having sex there too. I'll be honest — I couldn't help myself. I pointed out that by his logic, a prostitute was basically heaven's model citizen: someone who works *and* has sex simultaneously. I probably should have kept my mouth shut. But the more troubling part wasn't my wisecrack — it was what happened next.

When I raised the issue with other congregants, I was told that

I needed to go to the pastor and address it privately. He would hold court. I would come to him. There was no rebuke, no correction, no acknowledgment that something problematic had been preached to the entire congregation as truth. Because the king said it, it became true — as though it carried the same authority as something Jesus actually said. That's not a quirk of one bad church. That's the feudal system functioning exactly as designed.

And without accountability, heresy doesn't arrive with a thunderclap. It seeps in slowly, sermon by sermon, until a congregation can no longer tell the difference between what Jesus said and what their pastor *wishes* Jesus had said.

Target Acquisition

Now let's talk about money — because the feudal church is, at its core, a revenue operation.

The tithe is the castle's tax. And just as medieval lords assessed the value of their serfs' land, modern mega churches have become remarkably sophisticated at assessing the financial value of their congregants. Filmmaker Nathan Apffel, who runs the Religion Business documentary series, shared this account from a former church employee who worked in the "welcome" department of a large mega church:

She was instructed to collect not just names and email addresses from first-time visitors, but home addresses. Those addresses were then run through an outside firm that pulled home equity data. If a household had more than $1.5 million in equity, the head pastor called them personally and invited them back. As Apffel noted, a former special forces contact put it plainly: *"In the military, we call that target acquisition."*

Let that land for a moment. The church that claims to follow a man who said the last shall be first — who spent his ministry eating with prostitutes and tax collectors and social outcasts — is running wealth screening software on first-time visitors to identify the ones worth calling back.

The poor, the marginalized, the struggling single parent who scraped together forty-five minutes to try church one more time? They don't get a call from the pastor. They get a follow-up email from a volunteer coordinator asking if they'd like to serve in the parking ministry.

The mega church pastor is an expert politician. He never says anything too controversial. He cultivates centrist, broadly appealing messaging. He invites NFL players to speak at special events. He builds campuses — not because the surrounding communities need more God, but because the growth-through-acquisition model he borrowed from the corporate world demands that they need more church. Jesus said he'd leave ninety-nine behind to find the one. The feudal pastor follows this principle only when the donor is a tier-one six-figure donor. Otherwise, the ninety-nine will be fine with a podcast link and a coffee shop loyalty card.

The nepotism is almost impressive in its brazenness. The mega church pastor hires his spouse, his son-in-law, maybe a cousin — and suddenly these family members are gifted teachers and theologians, their wisdom apparently absorbed through proximity to the king. The church becomes a family heirloom, passed down through generations of pastoral dynasties, while the congregation funds the inheritance.

God Saw This Coming

None of this is new. That's what makes the Ezekiel passage so devastating — it was written between 593 and 573 BC, and it reads like a description of a church you could walk into this Sunday:

"Woe, you shepherds of Israel who have been feeding yourselves! Shouldn't shepherds feed the sheep? You eat the fat; you clothe

yourselves with the wool; you slaughter the fatted calves, but you do not feed the sheep. You have not strengthened the weak; you have not healed the sick, you have not bound up the injured; you have not brought back the strays; you have not sought the lost, but with force and harshness you have ruled them. So they were scattered because there was no shepherd."

Scattered. That's the word. And scattered is exactly what the data shows — a third of Americans who used to attend church and no longer do. Not because they stopped believing. Because the shepherd stopped feeding the sheep and started feeding himself, and eventually the sheep noticed.

Most pastors won't see themselves in this passage. The Pharisees at the time of Jesus were equally convinced they were doing it all for God. Sincerity is not a defense against self-deception — especially when the system you operate inside rewards exactly the behaviors Ezekiel is condemning.

Does It Even Work?

Here's the question the feudal church never wants to answer out loud: *Is any of this actually effective?*

It's effective at generating revenue — we know it can do that. It's effective at filling seats — it can do that too, for a while. But not effective at the one thing a church is actually commissioned to do: producing people who know Jesus deeply enough to help someone else know him.

The statistics we already looked at tell the story. Attendance has been declining for two straight decades. A third of formerly churched Americans are gone. Only 2 in 5 Christians are being discipled in any meaningful way—a staggering 95% of Christians who don't feel equipped to disciple anyone else.

The feudal castle produces excellent serfs. Loyal attendees. Generous donors. Reliable volunteers. But disciples? People who have genuinely encountered Jesus, who see the world through his lens, who are equipped to find their verse and scatter grace into other people's lives?

That's the job. That's the whole job. And by that measure, the castle is failing — not because the people inside it don't care, but because the system they're inside was never actually built for that purpose.

The question worth sitting with isn't whether you should leave your church. It's whether your church is building something worth staying for.

Translations and Mistranslations

The Bible is the most cited, most weaponized, and most selectively read document in human history. Churches will throw it at you like a fastball — but which verses they choose to throw, and which ones they quietly pocket, tells you everything about what they're actually trying to accomplish.

Before I go further, let me be clear about where I stand, because this section could easily be misread as an attack on the Bible itself. It isn't.

I believe the Gospels contain the word of God because Jesus spoke them. I believe he performed the miracles described there. I believe he was crucified, died, and resurrected. I believe the prophets spoke the word of God. I believe the Old Testament reveals the true character and nature of God. I believe the Holy Spirit is the living presence of Jesus here on earth, in spiritual form. And I believe the Bible contains spiritual truths that, when understood correctly, can reorient your entire life.

What I don't believe is that the Bible is a single, unified moral rulebook that speaks with a single, consistent voice across every book, letter, and poem it contains. And that distinction — between the Bible as a collection of spiritual truths and the Bible as a divine legal code — is where most of the damage gets done.

The Bible Is Not Univocal

Here's the theological term you need to know: *univocal*. It means "one voice." Many churches operate as if the Bible speaks with one clear, consistent voice on every subject — that you can open it anywhere, extract a verse, and apply it directly to your life or someone else's without any regard for who wrote it, who they were writing to, or what was happening culturally at the time.

That's not how the Bible works. And if you've ever noticed two Christians citing scripture to support opposite positions and wondered how that's possible — this is your answer.

Paul's letter to the Galatians was written to address a specific crisis in a specific community. His letter to the Romans was written to address what was happening in Rome at that time. His letter to the Ephesians was written to a church wrestling with its own leadership problems inside a deeply patriarchal culture. These aren't contradictions — they're context. And when you strip the context away and treat every verse as a universal eternal command, you don't get clarity. You get a weapon.

Here's a concrete example. Ephesians 5:22-24 says this:

"Wives, submit yourselves to your husbands as you do to the Lord. For the husband is the head of the wife as Christ is the head of the church."

Then Paul writes this in Galatians 3:28:

"There is neither Jew nor Gentile, neither slave nor free, nor is there male and female, for you are all one in Christ Jesus."

So which is it? A woman subordinate to everyone, or a woman completely equal to everyone? If a church wants to control women, it reaches for Ephesians. If it wants to reflect the actual arc of Jesus's ministry — in which women were the first witnesses to the resurrection, in which Jesus consistently elevated women in a culture that treated them as property — it reaches for Galatians.

That choice is not neutral. It is a negotiation. And every church, whether it admits it or not, is constantly making that negotiation — deciding which passages to prioritize, which to contextualize, and which to ignore quietly. The question worth asking your church is: Who benefits from the choices you're making?

When women are excluded from leadership, their concerns get marginalized. The decisions that shape a congregation's direction get made entirely through a male lens. That's not a spiritual truth — that's a power structure wearing scripture as a costume. This example is one of the best for breaking into small gatherings rather than a destination where corporate managers make decisions.

So How Do We Resolve the Contradictions?

This is the question that trips people up — and it's the one most churches never bother to answer honestly. If the Bible contains contradictions, if it wasn't written directly by God but inspired by him and recorded by human hands, how can we derive anything reliable from it at all?

Here's the answer: the same way we'd verify anything else that happened before cameras existed. Eyewitness testimony.

Consider this. Can you prove you went to the park yesterday? You paid no fee, showed no ID, left no record. How would you make the case? Simple — you'd tell me that Mary, Tom, Alice, and Boyd were all there and saw you. If I interviewed them separately, they'd all confirm you were at the park. Mary saw you with someone. Boyd didn't. Boyd saw you with a basketball. Tom and Alice didn't mention it. Tom thought you stayed thirty minutes. Alice said you were there for two hours. Different details, different angles, same essential truth: you were at the park. The discrepancies don't disprove the event — they actually authenticate it. Witnesses who agree on every single detail are usually rehearsed. Witnesses who agree on the core facts but differ on the edges are usually telling the truth.

That's exactly what you find in the four Gospels.

Very few people in the ancient world were literate. Stories traveled by mouth — told, retold, memorized, and passed from one person to the next before anyone wrote them down. Matthew was literate, so he wrote his own Gospel. Mark — whose full name was John Mark — was a close associate of the apostle Peter. He didn't witness Jesus's ministry directly; he wrote down what Peter told him. His Gospel and Matthew's overlap significantly, with small but honest discrepancies, exactly what you'd expect from two accounts drawing on related but distinct sources. Luke never met Jesus either. He compiled his Gospel from a careful investigation of eyewitness accounts and early followers — essentially what we'd call sourced journalism today. John was literate and wrote his own account directly. Four authors. Four perspectives. All are highly correlated with the central facts. Minor differences on the edges.

Those minor differences are a feature, not a bug. They're the fingerprints of real human witnesses telling the truth as they experienced it — not a committee polishing a consistent official narrative.

The same principle applies to the epistles. Paul wasn't writing universal policy memos. He was writing letters to specific churches, addressing specific problems within specific cultures. Of course, they differ from each other. A letter written to a church in Rome, navigating its relationship with Jewish law, will sound different from a letter written to a church in Galatia being infiltrated by legalists. Context isn't a loophole — it's the whole point. Strip the context, and you don't get the text's truth. You get a misquote dressed up as scripture.

So yes — the Bible contains tensions. It contains passages that seem to contradict each other. But when you read it as what it actually is — a collection of eyewitness accounts, inspired letters, prophetic writings, and wisdom literature, all pointing toward the same God who showed up in human form — the contradictions resolve. Not perfectly. Not always neatly. But honestly. And honesty is more than most institutions are willing to be.

The Rapture That Never Was

Here's one of the most widespread biblical mistranslations in modern Christianity, and it affects millions of people who have no idea it was essentially invented in the 19th century.

The Rapture — as depicted in the wildly popular *Left Behind* series, where believers vanish mid-sentence, planes crash because their pilots have disappeared, and the world descends into apocalyptic chaos — is not an ancient Christian doctrine. It was developed by a British theologian named John Nelson Darby around 1830. Darby took a passage from 1 Thessalonians 4:17, in which Paul describes the dead being resurrected. The living being "caught up in the clouds" to meet Jesus in the air, and built an entire eschatological framework around it — one that required conflating it with the Old Testament book of Daniel in ways that would have baffled the people Paul was actually writing to.

Because here's what Paul's first-century readers would have

actually pictured: walled cities. Kings returning from distant campaigns. The gates were thrown open, crowds streaming out to meet the king in the road and escort him back in. Paul was using a common cultural image of triumphant return, not describing a secret disappearance event. The direction of travel in his imagery is down, not up. Jesus descends. His followers rise to meet him and accompany him back. It's a welcome procession, not a vanishing act.

Does this matter? Enormously. Because the Rapture, as Darby conceived it and as mega churches have enthusiastically promoted it, is a remarkably effective fear-based conversion tool. Believe now, or get left behind. It also conveniently positions the church as the gatekeeper to your cosmic escape plan — which, as we've established, is exactly the kind of leverage a feudal institution finds useful.

The Tithe: An Old Covenant Tax in New Covenant Clothing

Speaking of leverage — let's talk about the tithe.

The 10% giving requirement is Old Testament law. It belongs to the covenant God made with Israel, the same covenant that also included dietary restrictions, animal sacrifices, and dozens of other commands that virtually no modern church observes. Jesus didn't abolish the Old Testament — he fulfilled it and established a New Covenant in its place. That New Covenant does not include a mandatory 10% tax.

Paul addresses this directly in 2 Corinthians 9:7: *"Each one must give as he has decided in his heart, not reluctantly or under compulsion, for God loves a cheerful giver."* Not a compelled giver. Not a guilted giver. Not a giver who's been told that withholding their tithe is robbing God. A cheerful one.

Yet the tithe is the one Old Testament law that virtually every denomination — regardless of how progressive or conservative their theology — has chosen to preserve. The Megas won't touch it. The PLUMBERS cling to it. Even churches that have jettisoned slavery, dietary laws, and Sabbath restrictions without a second thought will still preach the 10% from the pulpit with complete conviction.

Why? Because the castle needs revenue. And it turns out that framing generosity as a divine obligation is significantly more lucrative than inviting people to give freely from the heart.

The Thief on the Cross

If you want to understand what the Bible actually teaches about grace — not what churches have built around it, but what Jesus himself demonstrated — look at the thief on the cross.

It's Good Friday. Jesus is being crucified between two criminals. One of them mocks him. The other one — a man who has spent his life taking from people, mugging, bludgeoning, who woke up that morning knowing he would die for his crimes — says simply: *"Jesus, remember me when you come into your kingdom."*

Jesus answers: *"Truly I tell you, today you will be with me in paradise."*

That's it—no confession booth. No baptism. No membership class. No tithing record. No church attendance. No approved theology. No rosary. No penance. No speaking in tongues. Not even a prayer that followed the right format. Just a dying man, a desperate request, and a response from Jesus that blew every religious gate clean off its hinges.

The thief on the cross is a theological hand grenade rolled into the middle of every feudal church's carefully constructed system of requirements and rituals. He met none of them. Zero. And Jesus put him in paradise anyway.

I sometimes imagine what would happen if that thief walked into a typical church today. The welcome team would collect his address. The financial screening software would flag him as low-value. He'd be handed a bulletin, pointed toward the seats in the back, and invited to consider joining the parking ministry. Nobody would call him personally. Nobody would ask what he needed. And by the second or third Sunday, he'd stop coming — another data point in the de-churching statistics, another person who tried and walked away.

But Jesus? Jesus saw him from the cross, in agony, and made him a promise.

That's the gospel the feudal church keeps accidentally burying under its programs and politics. Not because the people inside it are evil — most of them aren't. But because systems, once established, develop their own gravity. And the gravity of the institutional church has been pulling people away from that moment on the cross for a very long time.

The Bible, read honestly, keeps pulling them back.

Disciple Dysfunction

Jesus gave the church one job. One. And it wasn't building campuses.

Let's start with the commission itself, because everything in this section flows from it. Matthew 28:18-20:

"All authority in heaven and on earth has been given to me. Therefore, go and make disciples of all nations, baptizing them in the name of the Father and of the Son and the Holy Spirit, and teaching them to obey everything I have commanded you."

And Mark 16:15, even more direct:

"Go into all the world and preach the gospel to all creation."

Go. Make disciples. Teach them. Send them out. That's the entire job description. Not "build a great Sunday experience." Not "develop a robust small groups program." Not "acquire campuses and grow your brand." Go. Make disciples. Everything else is furniture.

So here's the question that should keep every pastor up at night: by that standard, how is the church actually doing?

The Barna Group has the answer, and it isn't pretty. Only 2 in 5 Christians are being discipled in any meaningful way. And a staggering 95% of Christians don't feel equipped to disciple anyone else. Read that again. Nineteen out of twenty people sitting in churches across America — people who have been attending, tithing, serving in ministries, singing in worship bands, volunteering in welcome centers — cannot do the one thing Jesus specifically commissioned the church to produce.

That's not a program failure. That's a mission failure. And it didn't happen by accident.

What Discipleship Actually Is

Let me define the term, because it gets thrown around so loosely in church culture that it's lost most of its meaning.

Discipleship is becoming a follower of Christ so completely that your decisions, your priorities, and your instincts begin to align with his. Not perfectly — nobody gets there — but directionally, consistently, with the Holy Spirit doing the heavy lifting on the days you can't. A disciple knows what Jesus actually said and did well enough to explain it to someone who's never heard it. They can defend their faith not with rehearsed talking points, but with the kind of grounded, honest confidence that comes from having genuinely wrestled with the hard questions. They see the world through the lens we talked about in Chapter 4 — not the corrupted lens of a wicked world, but the lens Jesus offers. And crucially, they are equipped to help someone else do the same.

That last part is the whole point. Discipleship isn't a destination. It's a relay. You receive it, you grow in it, and then you pass it to someone else. That's how the first-century church grew from a handful of frightened people in a locked room to a movement that spread across the entire Roman Empire in a single generation — not through marketing, not through real estate, not through celebrity pastors, but through ordinary people who knew Jesus well enough to introduce him to someone else.

The church's job is to produce that. Instead, it mostly produces good church citizens.

The Difference Between Serving the Church and Following Jesus

This is where it gets uncomfortable, so stay with me.

If you are currently serving in a ministry at your church — pouring coffee, directing traffic in the parking lot, working the welcome desk, running the bookstore, volunteering in childcare — I want to be careful here, because your service is real and it matters to the people around you. But I also need to be honest: that is not discipleship. That is not your verse. That is church maintenance. And there is a significant difference between the two.

Discipleship is what happens when you sit across from someone who is lost, or hurting, or genuinely curious about Jesus, and you have enough of him in you to actually help them. It's what happens when your coworker's marriage is falling apart, and you don't just send them a podcast link — you show up. It's what happens when the person at the end of the bar is drinking their pain away, and you see them, really see them, the way we talked about in The Verse. It happens in kitchens and coffee shops, hospital waiting rooms, and in awkward conversations you didn't plan for.

Church ministry work can be a beautiful expression of your faith.

But the pastor-king who puts you to work in the bookstore isn't discipling you — he's staffing his operation. And when the church conflates the two, it produces Christians who are deeply loyal to the institution and almost entirely unprepared for the actual mission.

The current "Next" campaign model — so popular among the Megas — is a masterclass in this confusion. More church. More programs. More spaces. More access to the pastor's vision. What it produces is what I'd call a spiritual onlooker: someone who shows up every Sunday, watches the show, maybe joins a small group, and never actually picks up a racket. They've been watching tennis for years. They can tell you the score. They just can't play.

The Mission Less Mission Trip

Let's talk about mission trips, because this is where the church's discipleship failure gets most expensive — literally.

Some churches send their people, particularly their youth, on short-term mission trips to impoverished or war-torn regions. The stated goal is evangelism. The implicit goal, whether anyone admits it or not, is often a meaningful spiritual experience for the missionary. Both of those things can be true simultaneously, and neither one is inherently wrong.

But is it discipleship? Is it the Great Commission?

When I've asked people who've returned from these trips whether anyone was converted, the answer is almost always some version of "there was this one guy... but maybe." Satirist Taylor Ransom captured the absurdity perfectly when he described his first mission trip to the Bahamas — Hawaiian shirt, sunscreen, asking the church for more money to stay longer because they were "reaching people" playing volleyball on the beach. I thought it was satire until a local mega church posted an Instagram photo of its youth group at a beachfront restaurant in Cabo, with white linens and fine silverware. Captioned as a ministry.

Helping people in genuinely impoverished communities is good and righteous work, and excellent mission organizations exist that do it with integrity and real impact. I'm not dismissing that. What I am saying is that flying teenagers to a resort destination, calling it a mission trip, and funding it with congregant donations while two towns nearby are desperate for help is not the Great Commission. It's a vacation with a theological caption.

The Great Commission calls for people who are equipped, grounded, and ready to preach the gospel. Not onlookers who've had a moving experience in a tropical place. And producing those people — genuinely equipped disciples — requires the kind of sustained, intentional, one-on-one investment that doesn't scale well into a corporate model, which is exactly why the corporate church rarely does it.

What Encountering Jesus Actually Looks Like

When I ask churchgoers how they've encountered Jesus in their everyday life, the answers are almost always the same: "I prayed." "I served in my ministry." "I went to church." These aren't bad things. But they are, as I said, furniture. They keep Jesus at a comfortable distance — close enough to feel religious, far enough away to avoid being genuinely changed.

The Megas talk endlessly and intimately about having a "personal relationship with Christ." It's in their marketing, their sermon series, and their small group curriculum. But when you press them on what that actually means — what it looks, feels, and functions like on an ordinary Tuesday — the answers get vague. Because equipping someone for a genuine encounter with Jesus requires the pastor to get close enough actually to know them. It requires leaders who are spiritually deep enough to model what that encounter looks like. It requires a church that is more interested in your transformation than in your attendance record.

That kind of church is rare. But it exists. And it rarely looks like what you'd expect.

It looks like a small gathering. Ten, maybe fifteen people. Someone's living room. Honest conversation about what Jesus actually said, what it means, and what to do about it. Leaders who are close enough to notice when someone is struggling and bold enough to say something. A community oriented not around a Sunday experience but around a shared mission that points outward — into the neighborhood, the workplace, the relationships each person carries into the world every day.

That's the first-century model. That's what the Holy Spirit showed up at Pentecost to launch. And that's what the feudal castle, with all its programs and politics and capital campaigns, has been slowly replacing ever since.

The Goal Is God. Not Church.

Here's the honest summary of everything this section is trying to say.

The church told you the goal was the church. Show up. Tithe. Serve. Repeat. And if you did all of that faithfully, you were a good Christian. But Jesus never said the goal was the church. He said the goal was him. And the church — the real one, the living body of people who actually know him — exists for one reason: to help you get there, and then to help you bring someone else along.

If your church is doing that, stay. Fight for it. Help it do it better.

If your church is producing excellent serfs but almost no disciples — if it can tell you the square footage of its new campus but can't tell

you whether the people in its pews are actually being transformed —
then you have a decision to make.

Not about whether to follow Jesus. That decision was made on a
cross two thousand years ago, and it wasn't close.

But about whether the institution you're funding and serving is
actually helping you do it.

Discipleship Station

We've spent most of this chapter tearing things down. That was
necessary. But demolition isn't the point — it's the prerequisite. So
let's talk about what gets built in its place.

Paul lays the blueprint in Ephesians 4:11-13:

*"So Christ himself gave the apostles, the prophets, the evangelists,
the pastors and teachers, to equip his people for works of service,
so that the body of Christ may be built up until we all reach unity in
the faith and the knowledge of the Son of God and become mature,
attaining to the whole measure of the fullness of Christ."*

Read that carefully, because it contains the entire job description
of the church in three words: equip his people. Not entertain his
people. Not extract revenue from his people. Not build campuses
for his people. Equip them. Build them up. Send them out mature,
grounded, and capable of doing it for someone else.

Notice also what Paul says the goal is: the fullness of Christ. Not
the fullness of the church. Not the fullness of the denomination. The
fullness of Christ — meaning people who know him so well, who
have been so thoroughly shaped by his grace and his lens and his
mission, that his presence becomes visible in the way they live. That's
the target. Everything the church does should be measured against it.

By that standard, as we've established, the current model is failing. So what would a model that actually hits the target look like?

The Gathering

Start small. Radically, uncomfortably small.

Not a stadium. Not a theater. Not a repurposed warehouse with a coffee shop and a fog machine. Ten to fifteen people. Someone's living room. A kitchen table. The kind of space where you can't hide in the back row, where the person leading actually knows your name, where the conversation goes somewhere real because there aren't two thousand people watching.

The early church didn't start in buildings because buildings didn't exist yet — but I'd argue they wouldn't have wanted them anyway. What made the first-century gathering explosive wasn't its production value. It was its intimacy. People who actually knew each other, accountable to each other, praying for each other, challenging each other, and collectively oriented toward a mission that pointed outward. The Holy Spirit showed up at Pentecost in that kind of environment — and within a generation, it had spread across the known world without a single campus acquisition.

The small gathering can do everything the large church does. Worship. Communion. Teaching. Community. It can do all of it without the overhead, without the hierarchy, without the political machinery that inevitably develops when an institution gets large enough to have something to protect. And because the overhead is gone, the focus can go entirely where it belongs — on the people sitting in the room and what happens when they walk out the door.

This isn't a retreat from the world. It's a launching pad into it.

The Station

Here's where the model gets genuinely interesting — and genuinely different from anything most churches are currently doing.

Imagine that alongside the small gathering, embedded directly in the community it serves, there is what I'd call a discipleship station. Not a church building. Not a ministry program administered from a central campus. A station — a focused, specialized outpost positioned exactly where the need is, staffed by disciples who are equipped to meet it.

A caring station, for people navigating chronic illness, disability, or the quiet desperation of caring for someone who is. A hunger station, not a food drive administered from a distance, but a presence in the neighborhood, building relationships with the people it feeds. A bereavement station, for people in the wreckage of grief who need more than a sympathy card from a church they barely attended. A hospice station, walking alongside people in the final stretch of life with the kind of presence that no hospital protocol can replicate.

Each station has its own expertise. Each one is run by disciples who have been genuinely equipped — not volunteers recruited to staff a program, but people who have done the work of knowing Jesus well enough that his compassion flows naturally into whatever specific need they're addressing. The station isn't a church service. It doesn't have a bulletin, a band, or a giving talk. It has presence. It has competence. And it has the gospel woven into everything it does, not as a sales pitch but as the animating force behind why anyone shows up at all.

This is what it looks like to be rich toward God—not writing checks from a distance, not attending a service, and calling it engagement. It involves getting into the specific, unglamorous, irreplaceable business of meeting people where they actually are.

What This Asks of You

I want to be honest about what this model requires, because it's significantly more demanding than showing up on Sunday and putting something in the offering plate.

It requires you to know what you're equipped for. Not what ministry slot your church needs filled — what you actually bring. Your vocation, your experience, your particular set of wounds and recoveries, your specific way of seeing people. The bartender who understands loneliness. The nurse who knows how to be present in a room where someone is dying. The accountant who can help a struggling family understand why their finances keep collapsing. The person who lost a child can sit with another parent in that grief without flinching. Your verse, as we talked about in Chapter 9, is the intersection of what Christ has done in you and what someone else desperately needs. The station is where that intersection becomes tangible. That's why your identity in Christ – away from your default setting and your ideology- is so important.

It requires your church — or your gathering, or whatever you want to call it — to actually invest in equipping you for that. Not just preaching at you on Sundays. Not just enrolling you in a program. Knowing you. Walking alongside you. Helping you figure out where your specific gifts meet the specific needs around you, and then sending you out with the confidence and the support to do something about it.

And it requires a willingness to measure success differently. Not by how many people walked in the door last weekend. Not by the size of the building fund. By whether the people in your gathering are being transformed. By whether they're equipped. By whether they're finding their verse and living it out in ways that ripple into people you'll never meet and outcomes you'll never fully see.

That's a harder metric to track. It doesn't make for a great Instagram post. But it's the one Jesus actually cares about.

The Question Worth Asking

If someone took away your church's building tomorrow — dissolved the corporation, shut down the programs, turned off the fog machine — would the church still exist?

Would the people still gather? Would they still know each other deeply enough to keep going? Would they still be equipped to disciple someone? Would the stations still be running because the people staffing them were driven by something deeper than institutional loyalty?

If the answer is yes, you're in a real church. If the answer is no — if the building and the brand and the Sunday experience are what's holding the whole thing together — then what you have is a destination. And destinations, as we've seen, are exactly what the gospel doesn't need.

The church worth building is the one that functions just as well — maybe better — when the castle comes down. Small. Rooted. Equipped. Scattered into the world like seed, not assembled in a stadium like an audience.

That's the station. That's the model. And it's been available the whole time — buried under centuries of institution, waiting for someone to pick it up and use it.

Go find your station. Your verse is waiting there.

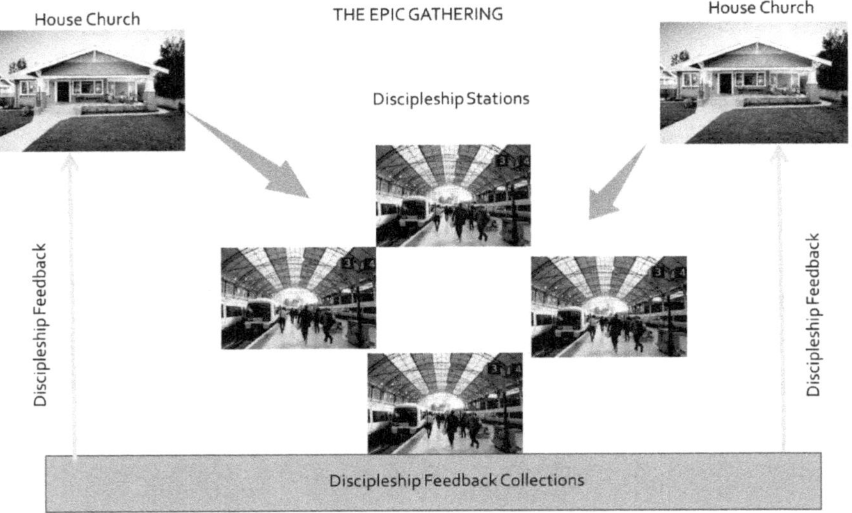

1. The house church serves as the base for future discipleship. This could be someone's house, a donated space in a commercial building. The gathering probably should not tithe to the house church. Only rent should be collected if needed. The house group does not have or support any ministries.

2. The house church is a place to worship, share experiences, learn through sermons, and participate in communion with Christ. The purpose of the house church is to help you find your identity, foster your verse, and send you out into the Powerful Play to do God's work. The house church is a station, not a destination.

3. The house church gathers and supports the discipleship stations. Funds are encouraged for the discipleship stations as needed. There is no tithe, as this is an Old Testament law, and we are no longer under it.

4. Examples of discipleship stations are caring for the poor, supporting mental health issues, as well as those families, encouraging those with terminal illnesses, etc.

5. A feedback loop back to the house church helps the house church nurture and support the discipleship stations.
6. The network allows multiple house churches to use the same discipleship stations.
6. I want to reiterate that this is just a paradigm. You can use this example to get your epic gathering started. Many small church communities are being developed as we speak. Simplechurchathome.com is just one of them. These sites offer resources for making disciples and growing spiritually.

188

EPILOGUE

So here we are. You have traveled through ten chapters of a book that was written for one reason: because the real Jesus — not the one handed to you by a controlling institution, a prosperity preacher, or a culture that has turned him into a bumper sticker — is worth finding. And because the people who walked away from him, or who never quite arrived, deserve an honest account of what they may have missed.

Let me try to say it simply, the way I wish someone had said it to me years ago.

Your soul needs to be connected to something that this world cannot provide. Not a better career, a cleaner conscience, a tighter community, or a more inspiring Sunday service. Something deeper than all of that. The restlessness you feel — the sense that there must be more, that the things you have been filling yourself with are not quite filling you — is not a malfunction. It is a signal. Augustine said it almost sixteen hundred years ago: our hearts are restless until they rest in God. He was right then. He is still right.

The invitation of this book has been to pick up the lens of Jesus and try looking through it. Not because you have to. Not because God is keeping score. But because the view from that lens is different from any other vantage point available to you — and because the life that comes into focus when you use it is the life you were actually made for.

Go through life holding two things at once: the brutal reality of the world in one hand, and the hope of eternity in the other. Do not sanitize the hardship or pretend the questions away. The storms will come. They come for everyone, the wise and the foolish alike, the faithful and the skeptical. What the foundation of rock gives you is not immunity from the storm. It is the assurance that you will still be standing when it passes.

Do not let the days go by. That is the quiet warning threaded through everything in these pages. The accidental life — the one that happens to you while you are not paying attention, the one that arrives at a destination you never chose — is the most common life there is. The examined life, the one built on something solid, the one oriented toward a verse in the Powerful Play, is rarer. And harder. And worth every bit of the effort.

Throw away the old Jesus — the one your church weaponized, the one your culture caricatured, the one who was supposed to fix everything and didn't. That was never him. The real Jesus does not offer a magic lamp. He offers a new direction, a companion for the road, and a foundation that holds. He offers the cross, which absorbs every failure and every shame and every "I should have known better" you have been carrying. And he offers the resurrection, which means that the last word on your story has not been spoken yet.

Your identity is not your default setting. It is not your ideology, your accomplishments, your regrets, or your worst moments. It is what is waiting for you on the other side of losing yourself — the self God made, recovered from a world that took it. That recovery is what following Jesus is for. It is slow. It is not always visible. It is the work of a lifetime. But it is real, and it is available to you right now, wherever you are starting from.

Your verse is waiting. The Powerful Play is already underway. You were not put here to be a spectator.

"Come to me, all of you that are weary and are carrying heavy burdens, and I will give you rest. Take my yoke upon you and learn from me, for I am gentle and humble in heart,

and you will find rest for your souls. For my yoke is easy, and my burden is light."

— Matthew 11:28–30

He meant it. He still does. Go find your verse.

192

ACKNOWLEDGEMENTS

I drew on many a pastor's teachings for this book, synthesizing and collecting their thoughts. I used the Stanleys: Charles and Andy, tirelessly watching and listening to their videos over and over again. I also borrowed from Tony Evans and Erwin Lutzer, as they are just fantastic.

I want to thank Mark Tusken for encouraging me to transition from a bunch of slides to a book:" Hey Mark, I finally finished it!"

The wrecking crew's original members, who taught me and provided the initial material: Daniel Nott, Omar Trevino, Kevin Holly, and Bob Haddad. I want to thank Gary Nielson, who first started this when he famously said, "Ya know, after 30 years, how come we don't have this right?" I want to thank Tom Rogus, who sat with me in a coffee shop after work, going through each slide and concept bit by bit.

Then my key reviewers: David Foxgrover and Charles Moore – thanks for putting up with an unedited version and your loving comments.

And last, but always first, Jesus, the "J" man and king. I can't wait to see you! Thank you for helping me write this book and putting these wonderful people into my life. This is my verse.

ABOUT THE AUTHOR

For most of his adult life, Joe Degidio tried to balance work, family, and faith while navigating churches that often felt political, corporate, or disconnected from the Jesus of the Gospels. A breaking point came when he realized that many Christians—himself included—could answer theological questions but couldn't explain why God allows suffering, what faith really is, or how to draw close to Jesus outside of rituals and programs.

That moment sparked years of study, discussion, and spiritual rebuilding alongside a group of seasoned believers he calls the "Wrecking Crew." Their conversations led to this book—a modern, honest, first-century approach to understanding Jesus.

Today, Joe Degidio writes for skeptics, wounded Christians, and anyone searching for a faith that actually brings rest, clarity, and transformation.

COPYRIGHT ACKNOWLEDGMENTS

Scripture Quotations

Scripture quotations are taken from the Holy Bible, New International Version®, NIV®. Copyright © 1973, 1978, 1984, 2011 by Biblica, Inc.™ Used by permission of Zondervan. All rights reserved worldwide. www.zondervan.com. The "NIV" and "New International Version" are trademarks registered in the United States Patent and Trademark Office by Biblica, Inc.™

Barbara Brown Taylor

Quotation from *Leaving Church: A Memoir of Faith* by Barbara Brown Taylor. Copyright © 2006 by Barbara Brown Taylor. Used by permission of HarperOne, an imprint of HarperCollins Publishers.

Jim Collins

Insights drawn from *Good to Great* by Jim Collins. Copyright © 2001 by Jim Collins. Published by HarperBusiness. All rights reserved.

The concept of the Stockdale Paradox is drawn from the work of Jim Collins and is referenced here for educational and illustrative purposes.

C.S. Lewis

References to the ideas of C.S. Lewis, including concepts from *The Screwtape Letters* and *Mere Christianity* and *The Great Divorce*, are made for commentary and educational purposes. The works of C.S. Lewis are copyright © C.S. Lewis Pte. Ltd.

The Wizard of Oz

Dialogue from *The Wizard of Oz* (1939), Metro-Goldwyn-Mayer film adaptation, produced by Mervyn LeRoy. © 1939 Turner Entertainment Co. Referenced for commentary purposes.

Poets.org

Definition of erasure poetry referenced from Poets.org, a publication of the Academy of American Poets. www.poets.org.

Walt Whitman

"Oh Me! Oh Life!" by Walt Whitman (1891) is in the public domain.

Every effort has been made to trace copyright holders and obtain permission to reproduce quoted material. The author and publisher apologize for any errors or omissions and would be grateful to be notified of any corrections that should be incorporated in future editions of this book.